T0268135

BLOODY PANICO!

BLOODY PANICO!

Or, Whatever Happened to the Tory Party?

Geoffrey Wheatcroft

VERSO

London • New York

First published by Verso 2024
© Geoffrey Wheatcroft 2024

1 3 5 7 9 10 8 6 4 2

Verso
UK: 6 Meard Street, London W1F 0EG
US: 388 Atlantic Avenue, Brooklyn, NY 11217
versobooks.com

Verso is the imprint of New Left Books

ISBN-13: 978-1-80429-575-5
ISBN-13: 978-1-80429-583-0 (US EBK)
ISBN-13: 978-1-80429-582-3 (UK EBK)

British Library Cataloguing in Publication Data
A catalogue record for this book is available from the British Library

Library of Congress Cataloging-in-Publication Data
A catalog record for this book is available from the Library of Congress
LCCN: 2024930771

Typeset in Garamond by Biblichor Ltd, Edinburgh
Printed and bound by CPI Group (UK) Ltd, Croydon CR0 4YY

Contents

Supercharged Champion

In the small hours of Friday, 13 December 2019, as the results of the general election came in, Alexander Johnson was in the Downing Street study. He had easily held his Uxbridge and Ruislip constituency but, as he watched more and more seats declare, he pumped his fist in the air while his adoring staff and colleagues embraced him. He had been leader of the Conservative Party and prime minister for less than five months but had managed to precipitate a general election by dubious and possibly unlawful means, to campaign on the slogan 'Get Brexit done', and to win the election with an outright majority of eighty seats over all other parties. This was the Tories' largest Parliamentary majority for more than thirty years.

It was a night of triumph comparable to another in 1867, when Benjamin Disraeli had thwarted a Liberal wrecking amendment to his Second Reform Bill in the small hours. At two in the morning he wrote to Queen Victoria and then went to the unofficial party headquarters at the Carlton Club, where he was greeted and toasted in words which the Tories might have addressed to Johnson on his own victorious night, as 'the man who ran the race, who took the time, who kept the time, and who did the trick'.

Both men were unlikely Tory leaders. Born in London in 1804, the grandson of Jewish immigrants from Italy, Disraeli almost accidentally became a member of Parliament, and a Tory, in that order. His father, Isaac D'Israeli, the delightful bibliophile and compiler of *Curiosities of Literature*, had been an unenthusiastic member of his synagogue even before he had a trivial row and departed, thereafter having his sons baptised in the Church of England. Catholic Emancipation allowing Roman Catholics to sit in Parliament wasn't passed until 1829, and the Jews Relief Act permitting elected members to take their seats without swearing 'upon the true Faith of a Christian' not until 1858; and so, but for Isaac's quarrel, his son would not and could not have been elected to Parliament until middle age. As it was, he stood three times before he was elected member for Maidstone in 1837, to his intense relief, since an MP couldn't be sued for debt.

He entered Parliament as a Radical, for want of anything else. With his very name and background, let alone his outré appearance – rings, ringlets, and fancy waistcoats, not to say his alarming record as a would-be speculator – he could never have joined the patrician Whigs. Even when he entered Parliament he was subjected to brutish abuse as a 'Jewboy' in the ever-unfunny *Punch*, and howled down in the Commons. And yet within ten years he was helping to bring down Sir Robert Peel's ministry when Peel was converted to free trade and the repeal of the protectionist Corn Laws.

Although Disraeli's conversion to protectionism was entirely opportunistic and unprincipled – in his later years of power he never thought of bringing back agricultural protection – this was his chance. He allied himself with the 'Young England' group of romantic reactionaries, whose quaint medieval revivalism he toyed with. His relationship with the very 'gentlemen of England' who had sneered at him not long before was transactional: they never thought that he was one of them, but saw him as an effective hitman, or professional in the cricket team, as one of those gentleman put it, who could provide the brilliance and bitter wit they lacked. Even so, although 'Dizzy's' scornful invective helped destroy Peel, it also helped divide the Tories, who were out of office for most of the next thirty years.

Like Dizzy, Johnson reinvented himself, beginning with his name. My opening sentence called him Alexander, which is his first given name, and the one by which he was originally known: his family and early friends still call him 'Al'. But he rightly thought that his second name was more striking and memorable, and so 'Boris' he became and remained, in a thousand headlines and endless adoring columns, even if it was in effect a stage name, like 'Lady Gaga'. If not quite an outsider as Disraeli, Johnson was nevertheless the great-grandson of a Turkish politician who had been lynched by an angry mob, and had other foreign ancestors besides.

He was also only the second British prime minister, after Andrew Bonar Law, who was not a native of the British Isles. Johnson was born in 1964 in New York, where his father was working. That made him an American citizen and he retained that citizenship for many years until he renounced it for tax reasons. An alternative history might be imagined in which he had entered American politics and wrought his havoc there instead.

Despite the classical education at Eton and Balliol that Disraeli had lacked, Johnson also remained something of an outsider, so that even when he was elected president of the Oxford Union or began working on *The Times* he was regarded with unease or suspicion, and not without reason. People who knew him at Oxford still recall the devious or underhand way in which he had campaigned for the Union. Later, his newspaper colleagues were aware from an early stage of his loose relationship with the truth, demonstrated when he was sacked from that first job for inventing a quotation. That didn't stop the *Daily Telegraph* from hiring him or sending him to Brussels, whence he dispatched a stream of fanciful stories about the European Commission and its plans to ban prawn cocktail–flavoured crisps or to decree that bananas should be straight (in shape rather than orientation).

But then a recording emerged of a telephone conversation in which a friend had urged Johnson to supply the address of a fellow journalist so that he could be beaten up: 'a couple of black eyes and a cracked rib or something like that'. Once again, he got away with it. He was given a dressing-down, but was allowed to continue as before because, in the unfortunate words of Max Hastings, his editor at that time, 'he was a peerless entertainer', as though entertainment rather than veracity were the main duty of journalism.

To be sure, that's what journalism's critics have always said, from Karl Kraus with his mordant definition 'A journalist is someone who has nothing to say and who knows how to say it' to J. F. Roxburgh, the English schoolmaster, who would sardonically return an essay to a pupil with the words, 'Excellent journalism, my dear fellow.' One of those pupils was Evelyn Waugh, who explained that by this phrase 'J. F.' meant 'trite in thought, colloquial in expression and aiming for effect by smartness and overstatement'. In Kraus's and Roxburgh's terms, Johnson was an excellent journalist. And he peerlessly entertained *Telegraph* readers with his descriptions of African children as 'piccaninnies' with 'watermelon smiles', and homosexual men as 'tank-topped bumboys'.

Both Disraeli and Johnson were sexual adventurers, more reckless, heartless and incorrigible in Johnson's case. Johnson conspicuously did not follow Disraeli's example as a youthful philanderer who became a happy and faithful husband. After a brief first marriage, his second, to the prominent barrister Marina Wheeler, lasted for more than twenty-five years and produced four children, before ending in acrimonious and expensive divorce, after years in which 'private life' was an altogether inapt phrase for Johnson, since his numberless infidelities, with their abortions and irregular offspring, were all too public. He has declined to say how many children he had and, to be fair, he may not know. In the *Doonesbury* comic strip 'Duke' hears the pious slogan 'Leave no child behind,' and remarks, as Johnson might have echoed, that that wasn't easy if you'd led his kind of life.

Again, like Disraeli, Johnson exaggerated his outlandish eccentricity, not least in appearance, although in an opposite sense. Instead of extreme dandyism, 'Boris's' shtick was a suit that looked as though it had been slept in, scuffed shoes, clumsily knotted tie, and an absurd mop of carefully messed-up straw-coloured hair. 'It must take a couple of hours of careful preparation to get all that right,' a colleague on the *Spectator* once said, and indeed after a make-up lady at a television studio had groomed him and lightly brushed his hair, he would immediately ruffle it up into what he thought his trademark haystack.

In one more similarity, both Tory leaders wrote fiction, joining an interesting list of politician–novelists which includes Winston Churchill, Joseph Goebbels, and Nadine Dorries. Although Disraeli's novels *Coningsby*, *Sybil* and *Tancred* are still readable, they are also silly. He was writing in a famous age for *romans à thèse* or didactic fiction, by Dickens, Newman, and Mrs Gaskell (not to mention Felicia Skene's novel of 1849 with one of the great titles, *The Inheritance of Evil; or, The Consequence of Marrying a Deceased Wife's Sister*). And by those standards, Dizzy can seem a frivolous poseur. *Sybil* contains one passage that entered the language. There were 'two nations; between whom there is no intercourse and no sympathy; who are as ignorant of each other's habits, thoughts, and feelings, as if they were dwellers in different zones, or inhabitants of different planets . . . THE RICH AND THE POOR.'

This somewhat trite recognition of the obvious was later turned into a slogan. In 1950, three Conservative MPs, Cuthbert Alport, Angus Maude, and Gilbert Longden, formed what they called the One Nation Group, its name a tribute to Disraeli, to deal with 'the willful inadequacy and inconsistency of thought and policy vis-à-vis the social services in the party'. Others joined them, including Enoch Powell, and the group was by no means easily placed on the left or right of the party. Or at least not until the 1980s, when 'One Nation Tory' became fighting words, used by such as Sir Ian Gilmour, invoking Disraeli's name in opposition to Margaret Thatcher's laissez-faire or slash-and-burn policies. But she routed and ousted Gilmour and her other 'Wet' critics in a milder form of Stalinist purge.

'History wars' were as vigorously fought in past centuries as now. The great struggles of the seventeenth century between Parliament and king were informed on the Parliamentary side by a popular although highly dubious version of history, about the ancient English constitution, in which there was no place for absolute monarchy. In the following century David Hume demolished this in his *History of England*, offering what might even be called a Tory version of history. But in turn Thomas Babington Macaulay tried to reverse that with his own *History of England* (1848–55), a masterpiece of English prose, and the classic exposition of the 'Whig version', in which the turning point was the Glorious Revolution of 1688 and the hero William of Orange, 'the Liberator' who had saved England from monarchical tyranny and papist reaction.

Although since viewed sceptically by both Marxist and neo-reactionary historians, this version has an undeniable basis in the fact that throughout the eighteenth century enlightened people in Europe gazed admiringly at England as the country that had overcome absolutism and clerical oppression, and had achieved some degree of constitutional Parliamentary government, rule of law and religious toleration. To be sure, this happened under a Whig oligarchy of great landowners, who proclaimed 'civil and religious liberty' but were at least as much concerned for the rights of Property, which they defended with a savage penal code.

When Disraeli tried to counter this, he cooked up his own version. He had already shown his gift for invented tradition when he devised his own family history, noble Hebrews who had once found refuge under 'the lion of St Mark' in Venice, a story which the Jewish scholar Cecil Roth many years ago demolished as complete fantasy. Then Dizzy proposed a version of English history – the Crown 'taken prisoner' by a cabal of Whig nobles – which is more claptrap. More entertaining than that are the passages of epigrammatic, camp paradox-mongering in his novels – 'There is moderation even in excess'; '"I rather like bad wine," said Mr. Mountchesney; "one gets so bored with good wine"' – of a kind that provides a link from Byron to Wilde.

And there is also a degree of self-knowledge. As Adam Kirsch has observed in his fascinating book on Disraeli, Dizzy's character Vivian Grey 'has all of his creator's charm, arrogance, and vaulting ambition, without any ballast of scruple or political principle', although not everyone thought or thinks that scruple and principle were ever Disraeli's salient attributes. In that very book he revealingly has his hero ask, 'Think you not, that intellect is as much a purchasable article as fine parks and fair castles,' and among his best creations are Tadpole and Taper, the time-serving placemen in *Coningsby*, for whom politics means quarterly incomes and principle means nothing at all. Johnson's own intellect would be, if not purchasable, then malleable and available for one purpose or another.

In 2004 Johnson published a novel called *Seventy-Two Virgins* – yes, he really did write a book of that title – in which he reveals himself more than he may have intended. Roger Barlow is a scandal-ridden politician who wonders whether everything might fall apart, and 'there would be nothing left for him to do but go on daytime TV shows. Perhaps in ten years' time he might be sufficiently rehabilitated to be offered the part of Widow Twanky at the Salvation Army hall in Horsham.'

Unlike his fictional alter ego Johnson hasn't yet played in panto, but part of his national fame came with his appearances on *Have I Got News for You*, a panel show in which wiseacres score off one another and make their guests look foolish. That was not difficult with Johnson, but he had already and very successfully illustrated the saying that all publicity is good publicity, and the more he played the clown the more some people liked him.

Although Disraeli was never a buffoon, he chose defiance rather than reticence as his method, and prospered. When Lord Derby became prime minister in 1852 for the first of three brief terms, he had no choice but to make Disraeli chancellor of the Exchequer despite private reservations about him. Dizzy's personal finances were not much of a recommendation. By the year after that triumphant reception of the Carlton Club, Disraeli had 'reached the top of the greasy pole', as he put it when he was appointed prime minister, and had begun to win the heart of Queen Victoria.

But in 1874 Disraeli won the general election with a comfortable majority, as Johnson would do in 2019. While Brexit – or a mood of national despondency and frustration at the impasse into which the referendum had led – helped Johnson win in 2019, behind Disraeli's victory at the 1874 election was a factor which would sustain the Tories for the best part of half a century. The Liberal Party, formed in 1859 from an alliance of Whigs, Radicals, and Peelites, or free-trading Tories, attracted much of its electoral support from the recently enfranchised commercial bourgeoisie and lower middle class. They were predominantly Dissenters or nonconformists, whose Methodist and Congregationalist chapels were ardently opposed to the demon drink, determined to restrict the sale of alcohol as much as possible, and maybe to prohibit it altogether. Gladstone recognised this. 'I have no doubt what is the principal' reason for defeat at that 1874 election, he told his brother. 'We have been borne down in a torrent of gin and beer.' Individual freedom is one of the very few things Johnson sometimes seems to believe in, and he would have been on the side of Bishop Magee, who told the House of Lords, 'Better that England should be free than that England should be compulsorily sober'.

But more than that, Johnson's ascent and regimen were characterised by his party's – and his personal – dependence on the support of rich donors, some of whom received peerages and other honours in return. During Johnson's brief tenure as party leader his connection to, and use of, such benefactors for private as well as political reasons would become scandalous. And there the comparisons end.

Borne up in that torrent of gin and beer, Disraeli served as prime minister for six remarkable years, ending as earl of Beaconsfield and knight of the garter, beloved of the Queen, revered by the Tories who had once sneered at him. Foreign policy apart, Disraeli's government, and particularly his home secretary, Richard Cross, did much for public welfare, with legislation to improve the housing of the working classes, to ensure better food, and to ameliorate the conditions of the masses generally with the great 1875 Public Health Act.

Two sharp contemporary reflections on Disraeli are pertinent. The Radical John Bright called Dizzy's ascent 'a great triumph of intellect and courage and patience and unscrupulousness employed in the service of a party full of pre-judices and selfishness and wanting in brains'. Much of that might have been said of Margaret Thatcher's 'great triumph' also, and yet only the personal 'unscrupulousness' and a party 'wanting in brains' applied to Johnson.

And in her splendid life of Lord Salisbury, his daughter Lady Gwendolen Cecil summed up her father's view of Disraeli, who 'was always making use of convictions that he did not share, pursuing objects which he could not avow, manoeuvring his party into alliances which, though unob-jectionable from his own standpoint, were discreditable and indefensible from theirs. It was an atmosphere of pervading falseness, which involved his party as well as himself.' John-son also made use of convictions he didn't share, above all over Brexit, and 'an atmosphere of pervading falseness' describes very well his time as prime minister.

With all that, there is in the end a vast chasm. Beacons-field died 'triumphant and full of victory', said one present at his deathbed, and his career could be described by Lord Randolph Churchill as 'Failure, failure, failure, partial suc-cess, renewed failure, ultimate and complete triumph.' Johnson knew failure, partial success and – as it seemed – complete triumph for a brief moment in the autumn and winter of 2019–20, when he won leadership and election, and boasted of a new dawn for the country. But within three years, he and his prime ministership ended in ultimate and complete failure.

That was not how it seemed as 2020 began. On 31 Jan-uary, the United Kingdom formally departed from the European Union. Talks with Brussels about how trade could continue were about to begin, and on 3 February Johnson gave a speech in the Painted Hall at Greenwich, Wren's magnificent building which was originally intended as a hospital for disabled or elderly sailors. His speech was meant to be a celebration of a new British liberty and a rhapsody about the glories of free trade, but then came a strange passage as if out of nowhere:

> To hear some bizarre autarkic rhetoric, when barriers are going up, and when there is a risk that new diseases such as coronavirus will trigger a panic and a desire for market segregation that go beyond what is medically rational to the point of doing real and unnecessary economic damage, then at that moment humanity needs some government somewhere that is willing at least to make the case powerfully for freedom of exchange, some country ready to take off its Clark Kent spectacles and leap into the phone booth and emerge with its cloak flowing as the supercharged champion of the right of the populations of the earth to buy and sell freely among each other.

This was pure 'Boris', straight out of one of his newspaper columns, jocosely casting himself as Superman against the 'doomsters and gloomsters'. There will be no room for gloom, he suggested, with no silly worries about a new threat to public health. True to that spirit, he took no action throughout February, and when March came, he went off with his family for the school half term to Chevening, one of the country houses available to senior ministers, where he was reported also to have been working on a book about Shakespeare. There was no warning about the danger of public gatherings. On 7 March he was one of 80,000 people at

Twickenham to see England play Wales in the Six Nations championship, boasting that he was still shaking hands with anyone and everyone. And the following week, the Cheltenham racing festival went ahead as usual.

Very soon many people, including some who had been at the rugby match and at the race meeting, were afflicted by a strange malady. Some were very ill, some died, and then more. In one European country after another all public places were closed, and people were told to stay indoors. Only on 23 March, seven weeks after the booster had derided the gloomsters at Greenwich, did Johnson announce a national lockdown, with the slogan 'Stay Home, Protect the NHS, Save Lives'. Johnson appeared on television wearing what he thought was a grave and serious demeanour but which always seemed to have a hint of a suppressed smirk, to say, 'You must stay at home. You must not meet your friends. If your friends ask you to meet you must say, "No".'

Within a little more than two years, the number of British people who had died of Covid-19 outnumbered all the British soldiers killed in the Second World War (and the American deaths outnumbered every American who had died in all foreign wars taken together from 1776 until today). Johnson himself was very gravely ill, and might have died. Instead, he recovered, but by the summer of 2022 he had been brought down and cast out by a rebellion of his own colleagues. This dramatic fall puzzled some observers and dismayed his curious band of devotees, but it wasn't hard to explain.

If Disraeli's relationship with the Tory party had been transactional to begin with, Johnson's always remained so, and his leadership was conditional. After the fall of Thatcher,

I was talking to Enoch Powell, the veteran if idiosyncratic Tory, who said, 'It's simple, really. A prime minister who loses the support of her cabinet cannot continue.' History repeated itself, now much more quickly. Johnson did everything he could to undermine his predecessor, Theresa May, whose prime ministership lasted only three years, but his lasted little longer than that, until the cabinet and Tory MPs decided that he was more burden than benefit.

He was bitterly resentful, and left Parliament, licking his wounds as he went off to make money. The Conservative Party's wounds were deeper and graver. Johnson was followed by the brief, calamitous but also ludicrous prime ministership of Liz Truss, who was ousted in turn to be replaced by Rishi Sunak, seemingly more sober and sensible than his predecessors, but not much more successful. When he was appointed prime minister, I sent half-ironical congratulations to a don at Lincoln College, Sunak's Oxford alma mater, who replied, 'We are very proud of Rishi and hope that he lasts at least a year.'

He did that, but as the new year of 2024 began, opinion polls consistently showed Labour with a large double-digit lead over the Conservatives, of a kind from which recovery was very hard to imagine. Those polls were confirmed by the real kind, a succession of by-elections in which Labour overturned huge Tory majorities, notably on 19 October 2023 with dramatic victories for Labour at Mid Bedfordshire and Tamworth.

That last was where in 1834 Sir Robert Peel had proclaimed the eponymous 'Tamworth manifesto', proposing that the Conservative Party, as he now called it, should move on from the antique Toryism of the Duke of Wellington and accept a 'careful review of institutions, civil and ecclesiastical', and 'the correction of proved abuses and the redress of real grievances', a most important stage in the party's development and a sign of its capacity for adapting to changed circumstances.

Those Labour by-election successes may not have owed much to the singularly uninspiring leadership of Sir Keir Starmer, whose own party was by that October troubled and conflicted over the latest bloodshed in Israel. All the same, looking at those by-elections and at those polls, there was no possible way the Tories could take away some positives, as football managers like to say after a defeat. The general election must come by January 2025 at latest, although realistically by the autumn. There was some speculation about a spring election, but as someone who had a successful and lucrative career in banking at Goldman Sachs, Sunak presumably knows how to assess figures and data.

Nor should Sunak be consoled by such veteran Tories as Kenneth Clarke and Michael Heseltine saying that it would be for the best if the Conservatives lost the coming election: best for the country, and for the Tories themselves. Their view is evidently shared by numerous Tory MPs who had announced they wouldn't stand at the coming election, some of them already making plans for lucrative careers after they leave Parliament.

All this was most remarkable considering the Tory party's extraordinary historical success. From Disraeli's victory in the 1874 election until 2024, the Tories were in office for 105 years out of 150 years, governing either alone or in some form of coalition or partnership with others – Liberal Unionists, Coalition Liberals, National Liberals, Liberal Democrats, even National Labour – whose fate was usually to be cannibalised and swallowed by the Tories. There is no political record in Europe which remotely compares with this. And yet by the second decade of the twentieth century it was possible to contemplate the party's demise, or at least drastic eclipse.

In 2005, shortly before the general election, I published a book called *The Strange Death of Tory England*, and was subsequently derided for that title when the Tories returned yet again, as they had done after losing by landslides at the elections of 1906 and 1945. In 1997 they suffered another historic, disastrous defeat, only to return to office in 2010, to remain there for more than thirteen years. But as I write, the title of my earlier book, to which this present volume is a coda or postscript, may seem to have been premature rather than entirely wrong.

This complete disarray into which the Tories have fallen is illustrated vividly by the duration for which the party leadership had been held. Lord Salisbury, Stanley Baldwin, Winston Churchill, and Margaret Thatcher had each led the Conservatives for roughly fifteen years. In the thirty-three years since the fall of Thatcher, the Tories have had nine leaders, including five prime ministers in the space of seven years. If 1936 was the year of three kings (George V, Edward VIII, and George VI), 2022 will be remembered as the year of two monarchs and three prime ministers, not to mention four chancellors of the Exchequer, five education secretaries, and more than thirty resignations from the government.

In a phrase often quoted, sometimes with irony, David Maxwell Fyfe, the barrister and politician who was the notably reactionary home secretary in the 1950s, said that 'loyalty is the Tory party's secret weapon'. Just how far from the truth he learned in the July 1962 'night of the long knives', when Maxwell Fyfe, by now Lord Kilmuir and lord chancellor, was among the third of Harold Macmillan's cabinet who were sacked in an attempt to bolster the prime minister's sagging position. Kilmuir's phrase was no truer sixty years later.

When Baldwin resigned as prime minister in 1937 he promised that he wouldn't 'spit on the deck or speak to the man at the wheel', words recalled by Harold Wilson in 1976 when he resigned and was succeeded by James Callaghan. More recent former prime ministers have by no means remained silent, although in Tony Blair's case, he didn't so much speak to the man at the wheel as jump ship. But Johnson was unique. Embittered rather than chastened by his ejection from Downing Street, sneering that 'when the herd moves, it moves', as if his own conduct had not driven that moving herd, he went on to spit in the face of the man at the wheel, explicitly or implicitly criticising Rishi Sunak.

At moments of turbulence within the party half a century ago, that grand old salt Rear-Admiral Sir Morgan Morgan-Giles would steady the ranks of his fellow Tory MPs with the words, 'Pro bono publico, no bloody panico!' At long last the Tories' ancient instinct for survival appears to have vanished, along with any concern for the public good, and bloody panico is the prevailing mode.

Tory England

Where did the Tories come from? The recent *dégringolade* of Conservative government and party cannot be understood without looking back at their origins and subsequent history. Something called a Tory party has existed in England for three and a half centuries. Indeed, the Tory historian Sir Keith Feiling took the story back even further and claimed that 'the first germs of Whig and Tory in England may be dated (like Florentine Guelfs and Ghibellines) from a wedding – the sacrament which united Henry VIII and Anne Boleyn and signalized our definite disunion from Catholic Europe'.

In origin the name Tory comes (with a certain historical irony) from the Irish Gaelic *tórai* used for an outlaw dispossessed by English settlers, thence a royalist or Roman Catholic rebel defying Oliver Cromwell's oppression, or a supporter of the Stuart crown. That first Tory party thwarted the Exclusion Bill that would have kept Charles II's Roman Catholic brother and heir, the Duke of York, from the throne, although that did not make the heir beloved of his people, or even of his natural supporters. And when he succeeded as James II it was only three years before he was deposed by the Glorious Revolution.

After fretting under William of Orange those first Tories had a final moment of glory during the reign of Queen Anne, the last Stuart monarch, with *émeutes* of High Church and High Tory passions such as the trial of the Oxford clergyman Dr Sacheverell, a 'high-flying' extremist who roused the rabble with the cry of 'the Church in danger'. But the Tories were defeated by the plain fact of the arrival and coronation of the Elector of Hanover as King George I of Great Britain and Ireland in 1714. They were forced to follow one logic of their position and become Jacobites, supporters of the exiled Stuarts, and to participate in two failed uprisings, in 1715 and 1745.

But the great majority of Tory country gentlemen and clergymen preferred resentful *innere Emigration*, accepting in practice the triumph of Revolution and Hanoverian succession, wondering, as A. J. P. Taylor would ask more than two centuries later, 'What sense had "Church and King" in the age of latitudinarian bishops and German princes?' Tory resentment was personified by 'the monks of Magdalen', the fellows of the Oxford college who taught or failed to teach Edward Gibbon.

Gibbon wrote that his time there was 'the most idle and unprofitable of my whole life', and said of those 'monks' that 'their conversation stagnated in a round of college business, Tory politics, personal anecdotes, and private scandal: their dull and deep potations excused the brisk intemperance of youth: and their constitutional toasts were not expressive of the most lively loyalty for the house of Hanover'. This might almost describe some other sodalities more recently such as Peterhouse, the Cambridge college from which, about forty years ago, the 'Peterhouse right' became celebrated as a centre of cerebral reaction or even bigotry.

With the accession of George III in 1760 the Tories' fortunes changed. William Pitt the Younger became prime minister in 1784 aged twenty-four and held office for seventeen consecutive years, which saw the French Revolution, the beginning of the Napoleonic wars, and political repression at home. The bloodletting of the Terror was eloquently denounced by Edmund Burke, and he has been claimed as an oracle, along with Pitt, by less intellectually backward Conservatives since, although some scholars have argued that both Pitt and Burke in truth remained Whigs.

In any case, if honourable English Tories wanted a patron saint they would do better to choose Johnson – the good and great one, not Boris but Samuel. In his *Dictionary* Dr Johnson defined 'Tory' as 'one who adheres to the ancient constitution of the state and the apostolic hierarchy of the church of England, opposed to a Whig', a definition which very much applied to him but has long since ceased to apply to most Tories. But with all his crankiness, Johnson was a noble spirit, and a comparatively infrequent example of how Tory attachment to tradition in church and state could be combined with deep humanity. In the century between Glorious Revolution and the risings of 1798 the mass of the Irish people lived in destitution under a veritable system of apartheid, with the country owned and ruled or misruled by the Protestant Ascendancy. Or as Johnson said, 'The Irish are in a most unnatural state: we see the minority prevailing over the majority.' He was repelled also by the cruelty and avarice of colonial conquest: his essay known as the '*Idler* No. 81' is as eloquent a polemic as anything by post-colonial thinkers.

Most of all, he abhorred the slavery whose profits may have fuelled the industrial revolution in England and certainly made numerous English families much richer. Johnson revered the monks of Salamanca who had demonstrated that slavery was incompatible with Christian doctrine. He saw the great canker in the heart of the American rebellion: 'How is it that we hear the loudest yelps for liberty among the drivers of Negroes?' a question that resonates until this day. And he drank a toast, 'Here's to the next rebellion of the Negroes in the West Indies.' Had Johnson said these things today he would be derided by the *Daily Telegraph* as a woke warrior and rabid Black Lives Matter fanatic.

Since Johnson died five years before the French Revolution he saw neither the long sequence of French and Napoleonic Wars, nor the reactionary repression of Tory governments in the 1790s, nor then after victory at Waterloo another period of extreme reaction under Tory governments in power until 1830, an age whose spirit was caught by Shelley in his savage 'England in 1819'.

An old, mad, blind, despised, and dying King;
Princes, the dregs of their dull race, who flow
Through public scorn, – mud from a muddy spring . . .
A people starved and stabbed in th' untilled field . . .
Golden and sanguine laws which tempt and slay . . .

His poem was dated the year of Peterloo, the butchery in a field near Manchester of peaceful demonstrators, much commended by the Prince Regent. In 1819, the Tory government passed its infamous Six Acts, strengthening the existing laws against seditious libel, increasing the onerous taxes on newspapers, restricting the conditions for bail, and hastening criminal proceedings, even though most trials at the Old Bailey lasted only a matter of minutes, often long enough for the accused to be sentenced to be hanged by the neck until he – or she, not to say a child – was dead. No one could have guessed that those wretched Six Acts would find an echo in the deplorable Five Acts passed by Boris Johnson's short-lived administration.

Forlorn radicals and liberals might for a moment have thought that England was doomed to ever-increasing repression of the kind seen on the continent at the time, the age of the ill-named Holy Alliance between the despotic powers of Russia, Prussia, and Austria. That didn't happen, and it was now that the Tories began, slowly at first, to display their remarkable guile, tenacity, and, above all, adaptability, their capacity for shape-shifting and chameleon-like knack of taking on the latest colouring.

Those long years of domestic reaction and repression had seen England transformed by the industrial revolution, and the change from a society based on rank to one based on class. E. P. Thompson wrote a classic book on *The Making of the English Working Class*, but another book could be written on 'The Making of the English Middle Class', and it was to this new reality that the Tories adapted themselves. To strengthen the party, the old landowning elite compromised first with the nascent commercial bourgeoisie, then the new 'captains of industry'. G. M. Trevelyan, the Whig historian, said that if French nobles had learned to play cricket with their peasants there would have been no Revolution. That might sound laughable, but it's not so different from Marx's sardonic observation that in France the bourgeois cut off their aristocrats' heads; in England they married their daughters.

That flexibility had a political aspect also. Within a couple of generations of the Six Acts, Bismarck could propound his rule of English politics, that progressive administrations took office to enact reactionary measures while reactionary administrations took office to enact progressive measures. In the latter case he was thinking particularly of Catholic Emancipation in 1829, repeal of the Corn Laws in 1846, and the extension of the franchise by the Second Reform Act in 1867. On each occasion a Tory ministry passed a crucial measure with support from the Parliamentary opposition against its own dissidents. One other measure might have been enacted in this way, and it was a tragic missed opportunity.

When Peel proposed the name of 'Conservative' for his party, it was a way of gently moving away from intransigent *ancien régime* Toryism, while suggesting that the party could conserve as much as possible of the existing order while adapting itself to inevitable change. In Giuseppe di Lampedusa's *The Leopard*, written more than a hundred years after Peel spoke, there is an oft-quoted line which might have been the Conservatives' motto: 'If we want everything to remain as it is, everything must change.' To be sure there were always spirits of true Tory reaction, from Lord Eldon early in the nineteenth century, who said that all change was change for the worse including change for the better, to Lord Salisbury at the end of the century with his principle that 'Whatever happens will be for the worse, and therefore it is in our interest that as little should happen as possible.'

From the 1980s, younger supposedly intellectual Tories began to make a puzzling cult of Salisbury, with a journal

called *Salisbury Review* and an admiring biography by
Andrew Roberts. He dedicated the book to Margaret Thatcher,
'thrice-elected *illiberal* Tory', attempting to link the two by
way of quoting Salisbury's self-description. But this is plainly
wrong. So far from Salisbury's principle of reaction, or
merely inaction, it was her instinct to make as much happen
as possible. Even if they led the same party, there was a vast
gap between Salisbury and Thatcher. He derided 'villa Conservatism', meaning the suburban middle classes who now
supported his party. What would he have made of the 'C1s',
in sociological jargon, the newly prosperous upper working
class and lower middle class for whom Thatcher had such an
affinity, and to whom she owed so much electoral success?

If the name 'Tory' survived, it was partly as a colloquial
alternative to 'Conservative' (or for some years around the
turn of the twentieth century 'Unionist'), useful for its brev-
ity, if nothing else, although also because some romantics
such as Iain Macleod preferred the name. But by whatever
name, the Tories would not have survived and prospered as
they did had they only followed Eldon and Salisbury. It may
be that, between the reigns of Charles II and Charles III, the
party was the political equivalent of the proverbial Stradi-
varius violin, which has been repaired so often none of the
original wood survives. There will always be a party standing
for property and invoking tradition, and we might as well
call them the Tories.

While Salisbury detested franchise extension, or indeed
anything that smacked of democracy, he quite failed to see
what was happening. His relations with two other Tories
were uneasy. Lord Randolph Churchill followed Disraeli by
preaching 'Tory democracy', a phrase which also repelled

Salisbury, and which Churchill himself said was 'largely demagoguery', but that was in a sense too modest. Disraeli and Churchill might both have been part-charlatan, but they had stumbled on a vital truth. Proudhon's 'universal suffrage is counter-revolution' was a little sweeping, but it turned out that popular parties of the right as well as the left could flourish under a universal electorate. It was traditional bourgeois liberalism that was doomed by the irruption of the masses into politics. In one of his speeches berating Peel in 1845, Disraeli said that Peel had 'caught the Whigs bathing, and walked away with their clothes', but that was what Disraeli himself did in 1867 with his franchise extension, and then as prime minister with the welfare reforms of his 1874–80 government.

Although the extension of the British franchise briefly helped the Liberals, it also produced that figure who would perplex the left for so long, the working-class Tory. Another cause of perplexity is often found to this day in such places as the *Guardian* comment pages: a supposed scission within the 'progressive' ranks. Tory political dominance for so much of the past hundred years is explained, or explained away, by the way that the anti-Tory vote was split between Liberals and Labour in the early decades of the twentieth century and split between Labour and Liberal Democrats in the last decades.

This is historically false. Labour began not as an ideological party but as a pressure group. Keir Hardie was the party's first Parliamentary leader, and he said they were 'not a Tory party, a Liberal party or a Socialist party, but a Labour party': a single-issue movement. Just as the third party by numbers in the Parliament elected in 1906, John

Redmond's Irish Party, had the single purpose of securing Home Rule, so Hardie's Labour had as its purpose securing the interests of the industrial working classes and their unions.

His new-born Labour Party was, it's true, a coalition, of bodies such as the Social Democratic Federation, the Fabians and the Independent Labour Party, which were socialist but tiny, and the unions, which were huge but not socialist. In 1918, Labour did adopt a socialist constitution including the famous Clause IV, which only accelerated a rupture which was already coming. Even before the Great War David Lloyd George, loved and hated as the radical standard-bearer, had talked privately about a possible coalition government of Liberals and Tories to resolve the questions of the hour. After the war, he led what was ostensibly such a coalition, dominated by Tories. And he and Churchill, both still nominally Liberals, hoped to see Tories and Coalition Liberals merge more formally as a centre-right party.

By way of response, Beatrice Webb, whose husband Sidney Webb had drafted the Labour constitution, said that 'for us as Socialists the real enemy are the Liberals'. What that meant in electoral practice has been described by Ross McKibbin in *Classes and Cultures: England 1918–1951*. Between the wars there were two salient points: the Tories evidently commanded the electoral support of a large part of the working class, and Liberal voters, when forced to choose a party other than their own, generally preferred the Tories.

There was much more to it. However we analyse it, the stark reality entirely confuted what had been foreseen or predicted by so many progressives, Radicals, Marxists, and other socialists, certainly including Karl Marx himself and his great comrade. Friedrich Engels outlived Marx by twelve years, and spent his later years carefully computing the date when socialist revolution would come about. Many of the best minds of the next century were drawn to Marxism, and some of the keenest of those, from Rosa Luxemburg and Antonio Gramsci earlier in the century to Eric Hobsbawm and Perry Anderson later, devoted formidable intellectual energy to explaining why it hadn't happened.

For more than a hundred years Marx has been indicted for failure to see the strength of nationalism. He was right about many things, but never more wrong than when he said that 'the proletariat has no Fatherland'. Too often that's all the poor do have, as much of the twentieth century has demonstrated. But it was not just nationalism. Looking back towards the end of his life, the great French *politicologue* Raymond Aron said that it was a denial of the entire experience of the twentieth century to suppose that people would reject their passions in favour of their interests.

Like Engels, Sidney Webb tried to predict the future by careful computation, claiming after 1918 that a mathematical graph showed that Labour must soon take office by democratic election. It was true that by the 1929 election Labour had overtaken the Liberals to run neck-and-neck with the Tories. This was before forming a second minority government while expecting to win a Parliamentary majority at the next election. Yet events supervened in the form of the financial crash and the subsequent Labour ruptures. This almost destroyed Labour, or so it seemed. From 287 Parliamentary seats they were reduced to a rump of fifty, and at that election and subsequent election in 1935 the Tories with their sundry appendages won more than half of the popular vote.

And yet during this interwar period the Tories were far from a party of mere reaction. Maybe the least successful member of Baldwin's 1924–29 cabinet was Churchill, serving most inappropriately as chancellor of the Exchequer, and he took the disastrous decision in 1925 to return to the gold standard at the prewar rate. This was followed by his hectoring class war during the 1926 General Strike, which reconciled him to the right wing of the party, which had hated him ever since he had deserted the Tories in 1904. By contrast, the outstandingly successful member of that government was Neville Chamberlain, who declined Baldwin's offer of higher post to become minister of health, and changed the country. His achievements, from housing to healthcare and much else, were simply heroic.

Whether Chamberlain should really count as a Tory is another matter. Political allegiances in England have often been fluid or transient. Gladstone was first elected to Parliament as the 'rising hope of those stern and unbending Tories', in Macaulay's phrase, defending his father's 'West Indian interest', which is to say slavery, and ended as 'the people's William', adored by cottagers and miners and execrated by Queen Victoria. Churchill turned his coat not once but twice, deserting the Tories for the Liberals as they were in the ascendant and then deserting them in turn twenty years later as they declined.

As to Chamberlain, he disliked that name 'Conservative', and used playfully to tell his Birmingham constituents (echoing Gilbert and Sullivan) that he was not 'born a little Conservat-eyve' but born a Liberal and brought up a Liberal

Unionist following his father's tergiversations, and when he died, a family friend, Lady Debenham, wrote to his widow, 'Neville was a Radical to the end of his days. It makes my blood boil when I see his "Tory" and "Reactionary" outlook taken as a matter of course because the Whirligig of Politics made him leader of the Tory Party.'

This was only one example, although a very striking one, of the Tories' flexibility. Sometimes committed to free trade, sometimes protection, now determined to crush Irish rebels, now to making terms with them, routing the trade unions in the 1920s but placating them in the 1950s before routing them again in the 1980s. And the Tories showed a remarkable gift for recovering from disaster. Having been thrashed by the Liberals in 1906, the Tories came back to hold office, alone or in coalition for all but three years during the three decades from 1915 to 1945.

That last saw an election held when the greatest war in human history had just ended in which the warring powers had conscripted and directed scores of millions of people in unprecedented fashion. Indeed, the war may have been the nearest England ever came to totalitarianism, with state direction of labour and capital, police control of personal finance, censorship of the press, imprisonment without trial, and forced labour in the mines (the 'Bevin boys'). Planning and 'controls' were accepted as part of the new way of life by the 'Socialists of all parties' to whom Friedrich Hayek half-ironically dedicated his libertarian polemic *The Road to Serfdom*.

Churchill had either read or been told about this book before he made his calamitous election broadcast in July 1945, in which he disgracefully warned that Labour government would mean 'some kind of Gestapo'. And yet the Tories, in opposition until 1951 and then in office, accepted a great deal of what the Attlee government had done, from the nationalisation of coal-mining and railways to the National Health Service.

If the Tory governments of 1951 to 1964 weren't particularly successful, the Conservative and Unionist Party as an institution most certainly was. Its membership had grown steadily between the wars and by the early 1950s it reached an astonishing 2.8 million members. There were individual Parliamentary constituencies such as Barnet, where Reginald Maudling was first elected in 1950, with an electorate of 70,000 – and a constituency Conservative Association with more than 10,000 members. Commentators on the left looked at those figures in perplexity, compared them with Labour's membership, and concluded ruefully that the Tories had a stronger popular base than Labour. This memory would be both significant and poignant seventy years later.

In their simple but effective slogan at the 1964 election, Labour lamented 'Thirteen wasted years', and so they had been. A cynical Frenchman once said that England's misfortune was that she won the war. A physically and morally devastated Germany rapidly recovered, and soon overtook the victor in terms of economic innovation and productivity. Harold Macmillan boasted that the British had never had it so good, but other countries had it better, as Macmillan dimly realised. In 1963 he summoned his ministers to Chequers for what Iain Macleod, one of those attending, called a 'somewhat pointless planning meeting on the modernisation of Britain'. Its pointlessness summed up what the Tories had done, or left undone.

In terms of formation and background, the four prime ministers during those thirteen years seemed striking survivals of another age, all of them more or less patrician: Churchill, the grandson of a duke, Eden, the son of a baronet, Macmillan, the son-in-law of a duke, Alec Douglas-Home, the fourteenth Earl of Home until he renounced his title. One of them was educated at Harrow, the other three at Eton, and the first three had all served as infantry officers in the Great War. Churchill and Eden moreover became Knights of the Garter.

Despite all that, and the increasing derision heaped on that old order, the Labour victory at the 1964 election was surprisingly narrow: just over 200,000 out of more than 27 million popular votes, or less than one per cent. But this was still enough to discompose the Tories. And when Douglas-Home resigned the following year they went to the other extreme by choosing as a new leader Edward Heath, who was not only plebeian but remarkably graceless and churlish.

That began four decades in which the party was led by a long line of nonentities, more or less lower-middle-class men, a line electrifyingly interrupted 'by a woman who through character and conviction changed the country'. The words are Perry Anderson's in *New Left Review*, and it was notable how the importance and significance of Margaret Thatcher and 'Thatcherism' was recognised, and almost admired, albeit ruefully, by writers on the serious left such as Anderson and Raphael Samuel.

Having challenged Heath for the leadership in 1975 Thatcher defeated him and went to win an unprecedented three successive elections. That would be repeated by Blair, but much less impressively since the Tory popular vote remained steady at the 1979, 1983, and 1987 elections, while the vote for Labour, despite the party's managing to remain in office, declined and then plummeted over the 1997, 2001, and 2005 elections.

And Thatcher's government, like Attlee's but unlike Blair's, transformed the country. Much of Thatcher's work endured, and could still be seen as a victory for Tory democracy. This includes much wider ownership of houses and shares, together with a much lower frequency of strikes. But the deregulation of finance by the 1987 'Big Bang' transformed the City of London, and helped lead to the financial implosion two decades later. Meanwhile the privatisation of water provided a cloacal epitome of Thatcherism at its worst. Shareholders' pockets were filled with scores of billions in dividends while the country's rivers and seas were filled with excrement.

To this day Thatcher is misunderstood, misprized, and misappropriated, by her admirers even more than by those who revile her memory. It seems almost futile to point out that she voted in the 1960s for the liberalisation of divorce and abortion and the decriminalisation of homosexuality. She was called 'the milk-snatcher', when in fact as education secretary she opposed ending free school milk, and she was accused of destroying the mining industry, when more pits were closed during the seven and three-quarter years of Wilson's prime-ministerships than the eleven and a half of Thatcher's.

On one question in particular she has been totally misrepresented. When she died, Andrew Roberts wrote a eulogy in the *Wall Street Journal* claiming that 'her support for Israel was lifelong and unwavering', and this was echoed in late 2023 by the quaintly named Nile Gardiner (does he have brothers called Ganges and Danube?), a leading

Angloneocon who is director of the Margaret Thatcher
Center for Freedom at the Heritage Foundation in Washington. He wrote that 'Lady Thatcher had a tremendous affinity
with Israel', and added that she 'hated terrorism in all its
forms, whether it was carried out by the IRA, al-Qaeda, or
state-sponsored'. These were at best half-truths, if that.

When she became prime minister in 1979, the permanent
undersecretary of the Foreign Office was Sir Michael Palliser, and her first foreign secretary was Lord Carrington.
Palliser was talking one day to Shlomo Argov, the Israeli
ambassador in London, whose attempted assassination by
Palestinians in 1982 prompted an ill-fated Israeli invasion of
Lebanon. Argov said that Carrington, and maybe by impli-
cation Palliser as well, belonged to the patrician old guard,
whose disdain for Israel was underlain by a more traditional
prejudice. But the prime minister was quite different, he
said: she understood and instinctively supported Israel.

He could not be more wrong, Palliser told the ambassador. Carrington and Palliser had both been young Guards
officers in 1945, when they entered Germany in their tanks
and saw for themselves something of the horror the Third
Reich had inflicted on the Jewish people. As for Thatcher,
'She's the one who never misses an opportunity to mention
the sergeants.' They were the two young British conscript
soldiers serving in Palestine who were captured and hanged
in 1947 by the Irgun, the militia of the right-wing Revision-
ist Zionists. It was led at the time by Menachim Begin.

In 1977 he became prime minister of Israel, until 1983
when he was succeeded by Yitzhak Shamir, who held the
office until 1993 apart from a two-year interval. He had once
been a leader of Lehi, known to the British as the Stern

Gang, and in 1944 had ordered the assassination of Lord Moyne, Churchill's proconsul in Cairo. Thus for most of the years that Thatcher was in Downing Street, the prime ministers of Israel were two men she regarded as terrorist murderers. She did indeed hate terrorism in all its forms, whether Irish Republican, Islamist, or Zionist.

By the late 1980s even those few people truly devoted to her recognised her increasingly hubristic arrogance. Her private secretary was Charles Powell, technically an official appointment meant to give the prime minister detached advice, or even to keep her on the straight and narrow. But Powell become her *éminence grise*, closest adviser and warmest supporter, to the point where Sir Robin Butler, the cabinet secretary, threatened to resign if Powell remained. After that 1987 election, her third consecutive victory, Powell congratulated Thatcher, but added, 'all the same, I hope you will not put yourself through it again.' At some point soon, her 'reputation and standing as a historic figure' would matter more than anything more she might do. 'Your place in history will be rivalled in this century only by Churchill. That's the time to contribute in some other area!'

This clear intimation of her political mortality was seconded by Denis Thatcher, her husband, who urged her to leave at the latest in the spring of 1989, after ten years in office. She didn't, and the circumstances in which she was deposed in November 1990 had a disastrous effect on her party. Not long before her intensely dramatic departure from office, the veteran Conservative politician William Whitelaw was talking to Butler, who was taken aback by what he heard. 'The trouble is,' Whitelaw said, 'that when Margaret leaves, she will leave the Conservative Party divided for a generation.'

That proved to be all too true, and her downfall, or the way it was brought about, poisoned the Tories. Even those of her colleagues who recognised that she had outstayed her welcome and become a liability rather than an asset were repelled by the manner of her political assassination. Not long after her removal, the veteran journalist Paul Johnson, a fiery radical turned angry reactionary, was talking to a Tory MP, who said, 'I'm afraid this means we've become a party of cowards.'

'And shits.'

'Oh, we've always been that!'

That exchange would echo over many years to come.

Thatcher's Heirs

And yet Thatcher's effect on her own party was scarcely greater or more important than her longer-term effect on the opposition. In some ways her most remarkable achievement could be seen by way of her successors at 10 Downing Street. Thatcher might be gone, but her -ism survived. Simon Jenkins's book *Thatcher and Sons* describes how those political sons and heirs, John Major, Tony Blair, and Gordon Brown, all implicitly accepted Thatcher's legacy in terms of political economy, while she herself quite rightly came to see Blair as her greatest achievement.

He picked up Bill Clinton's inane jargon of 'the third way', sardonically defined as 'the left got the words and the right got the deeds', something the cheerleaders of New Labour failed to see then or later. Will Hutton was one of the more effusive of those cheerleaders. His book *The State We're In* enjoyed a great success at least with the chattering classes, vaguely progressive academic and media folk, and in the spring of 1997 he followed it with a flag-waving manifesto for the glorious Labour government that awaited, promising, 'A new agenda for Britain.' It received an extremely sharp and funny review in the *Spectator* by

Robert Taylor, *Financial Times* journalist and a man of the left (not such rare combination): 'Poor Will Hutton is going to be very disappointed with the New Labour after 1 May [election day] . . . he seems to believe that we are on the eve of "the strange rebirth of liberal England".' Very soon the country would be changed by this new government, by way of higher taxes and a renewed relationship with the unions, leading to 'a new formulation of Middle England, which could underpin a progressive political coalition for decades'.

To which Taylor could only say, 'How New Labour's callow young spin doctors in Millbank Tower must be laughing among themselves at such patent absurdity. They know from their own focus group findings that what Middle England really, really wants is Thatcherism with a fresh young face and this is what Mr Blair provides it with.'

And yet this imitation, that sincerest form of flattery, was a problem for the Conservatives. It had been a familiar pattern of British politics for one party to outplay another by appropriating its policies, but there had never been such a stealthy appropriation as this, and its electoral effect has been overlooked. In 1997 much nonsense was talked and written about the 'revolutionary times' we lived in, which was precisely what they were not. Blair's gift was to say 'Time for a change' while making it clear that nothing very important would change. He and his party won a landslide that year, at least in terms of Parliamentary seats, but the victory needed deconstructing.

Over the previous five years Tories had been consumed by fratricidal strife. After the victory of John Major's Tories at the May 1992 election, which surprised so many, his authority was gravely damaged by 'Black Wednesday' the following September. Sterling was forced out of the European Exchange Rate Mechanism by an advanced form of bear squeeze that saw investors, notably George Soros, making huge profits by speculating against the pound. At the same time a group of Europhobic backbenchers had conducted a guerrilla campaign against ratification of the Maastricht treaty. Even inside the cabinet there were refractory ministers, the 'bastards' as Major called them at the end of a television interview when he thought the microphone was turned off.

In May 1997 the bedraggled and demoralised Tories saw their vote collapse, from 14 million in 1992 to 9.6 million. New Europhobic parties had sprung up and had won getting on for a million votes: 811,849 for the Referendum Party led by the sulphurous figure of Sir James Goldsmith, and the United Kingdom Independence Party or Ukip with 105,722. It may be supposed that almost all of these were defecting Tory voters, and in the euphoria of the hour few noticed that triumphant Labour had actually won fewer popular votes than the Tories five years earlier. Then the electoral system played its usual tricks. Party leaders in countries with proportional voting would be astonished by an election at which the victorious party gained 64 per cent of Parliamentary seats with no more than 43 per cent of the popular vote.

And finally there was a curiosity: the Liberal Democrats doubled their number of Parliamentary seats, with a smaller vote. This could only mean that the British had discovered for the first time since the 1920s the art of tactical voting:

millions of people were not voting *for* New Labour – or the Lib Dems or Referendum Party – so much as *against* the Tories. The British didn't want to become a 'democratic one-party state', like Italy for many years under the Christian Democrats or Japan seemingly forever under the Liberal Democrats (in no way whatever to be confused with the British party of the same name). The country was fed up with the Tories, the Tories were fed up with themselves, and Blair's victory was largely negative.

In 2001 Labour were re-elected but the most remarkable fact that year was voting turnout. The British were once enthusiastic voters, as citizens of other countries remained. The highest turnout in any British general election was 84 per cent in 1950. Turnout remained in the upper 70s per cent mark through the years of Thatcher's supremacy and on until 1997, when it fell to 72 per cent. While that figure dismayed some observers, they may also have sensed over the following four years that it could fall again. But no one foresaw the collapse to 59 per cent, which may have been Blair's most significant political achievement. By 2001, voters were faced with a choice between William Hague, a Conservative who couldn't win, and Blair, a conservative who could. Re-electing the Blair government was understandable enough in those circumstances, but four out of ten citizens drew another logical conclusion and didn't bother to vote at all.

What Blair had done was perceived by one of his earliest supporters, the political journalist turned novelist Robert Harris. In 2004 he wrote in the *Daily Telegraph* a somewhat backhanded tribute on the tenth anniversary of Blair's election as Labour leader:

Right-wing in his instincts even before he became party
leader, Blair has clearly moved further to the Right since
entering Downing Street . . . On crime, education and
health, he has shamelessly filched the rhetoric – and in
some cases even the policies – of his Tory opponents . . .
if Blair did have a faction, it would probably not be on
the Left at all, but located somewhere deep within the
Conservative Party.

To illustrate this he quoted Charles Moore, a former editor
of the *Daily Telegraph* still writing a column for that paper,
who described Blair as 'prescient, brave, eloquent and in
charge . . . a prime minister not just a party leader'.

That was written a year after Blair had led the country
into a criminal and catastrophic war by way of shameless
deception in support of the most right-wing American
administration in memory, whose motives for the invasion
of Iraq were not shared by most British people and certainly
not by almost any of the Labour MPs who cravenly voted
for it. This dismal episode is illuminated by a comparison.
Although they weren't of course identical, there were striking similarities between the Suez escapade of 1956 and the
Iraq war of 2003.

On both occasions Western governments were enraged
by an Arab dictator and wished to be rid of him. In 1956
the French believed Colonel Gamal Nasser of Egypt was
fomenting the insurrection in Algeria (which wasn't true
since it needed no outside stimulus). The British hated Nasser
because he had expelled their army and was proposing to
nationalise the Suez Canal. And the Israelis knew him as
their greatest enemy. Likewise, by the beginning of the next

century the administration of George Bush the Younger in Washington was determined to be rid of Saddam Hussein, the ruler of Iraq, and Blair was always game for any military adventure.

But on both occasions also, it was impossible for political reasons openly to avow that the intervention was for the purpose of what would come to be called regime change. And so, again on both occasions, the plotters conspired. Between the two episodes there was in the eighteenth-century sense a diplomatic revolution. In 1956 the British and French colluded with Israel in a plot which would see the Israeli army attack Egypt suddenly and apparently unbeknown to London and Paris. And then Anglo-French forces would intervene ostensibly in a 'police action' to separate the warring parties.

Alas, the rug was pulled from under the conspirators by the Eisenhower administration in Washington. In 2002–3 the collusion was between the Americans and the British, or more exactly between Bush and Blair, while President Jacques Chirac of France opposed the war. An outrageous story was fabricated about Saddam Hussein's connection with the 11 September attacks on New York and his supposed possession of 'weapons of mass destruction', on which Blair based his own case.

All of this represented a problem – and an opportunity – for the Conservatives, or should have done. However far-fetched it may seem, it remains a fascinating 'if' of history to speculate what would have happened if the Tories, while making the usual noises about sympathy for the Americans, had said that the case for war had not been demonstrated. The Suez adventure compared favourably with Iraq at every point, and particularly from a Tory perspective. For one thing, the Suez imposture was seen through almost from the start, whereas many people, as well as much of the media, refused to recognise until far too late the fraudulence of the claims on which the invasion of Iraq was based.

In 1956 the casualties suffered by all sides were not very heavy, whereas the Iraq war led to the deaths of hundreds of British troops, thousands of Americans, and hundreds of thousands of Iraqis. After Suez the political damage done was repaired quite soon and fences were mended in the Middle East. In contrast, the consequences of the calamity of Iraq will be with us for generations.

After Hague's thoroughly unsuccessful four years as Tory leader led to another electoral defeat, he resigned as leader. He might have been chastened, but his contribution to the Iraq debate was a particularly abject farago of nonsense which disqualified him as a historian as much as a statesman: 'Whenever we really need help, we turn to the United States of America, and Europe turns to the United States. Without America, France would have lived under dictatorship for decades . . . We turned to America, and our alliance with the United States is a fundamental attribute of the foreign policy of this nation when it is correctly conducted.'

Dismal as the original support of most Tories for Blair's war had been, they later had another opportunity to disassociate themselves from it. Within only a few years the sheer scale of Blair's deceit had become clear. In the Commons on 24 September 2002 he had claimed that the intelligence on Saddam's weapons of mass destruction was 'extensive, detailed and authoritative'. It was now learned that what the Joint Intelligence Committee had actually told him was that the available evidence was 'sporadic and patchy' and 'remains limited'.

We also learned what Sir David Manning, Blair's foreign policy adviser, had reported on 14 March 2002 after conversations in Washington with Condoleezza Rice, Bush's national security adviser. 'I said that you would not budge in your support for regime change,' Manning had written, 'but you had to manage a press, a Parliament and a public opinion that was very different than anything in the States.' Such a difference wasn't very surprising, since Blair, unlike Bush, had insisted that the war was not being fought simply for regime change, which his MPs would not have supported.

Then in May 2005 we learned of the report dated 23 July 2002 recording the exchanges between Sir Richard Dearlove, head of the Secret Intelligence Service or MI6, and his counterparts in Washington, which read, 'The intelligence and facts were being fixed around the policy.' This entirely demolished Blair's claim that a decision for war had not been taken when it had, and thus any belief in his basic honesty and good faith.

Matthew Parris is a former Conservative MP who had served as an adviser to Thatcher, and for years past has written a column for *The Times*. He had been a fierce critic of the Iraq war and the neocons whose war it was, and he now urged the Conservatives to use all that had come to light about Blair's deception to dissociate themselves from the invasion, saying correctly that we had been taken to war on a false prospectus. Not only would this have been a principled stance, it would have been very popular, since few British voters any longer saw the war as other than a disaster based on a lie.

As Max Hastings has said, 'Churchill invented the con-
cept of the "special relationship" for reasons of political
expediency' before he became the first of many prime ministers who discovered that it didn't exist. A true and even
moderately patriotic Conservative Party would have seen
this and acted accordingly. But by now the Tories, or too
many of them, matched Léon Blum's phrase about the
French communists: as Blum said, the PCF was 'a foreign
nationalist party'; and so it seemed were the Tories.

At the 2005 election the Tories made a modest recovery,
but something else had gone wrong for the party, which
affects this whole story: the method of choosing its leader.
Until and including the shameless way in which Macmillan
had jobbed in the Earl of Home as his successor in October
1963, Tory leaders had 'emerged' after supposed 'normal
processes' of consultation. Sometimes there was an acknowledged crown prince, as when Chamberlain succeeded
Baldwin in 1937 and Eden succeeded Churchill in 1955, not
that those two successions proved very happy. Sometimes
the choice could be contentious. When Bonar Law resigned
with terminal cancer in 1923, some people thought that
Lord Curzon might succeed him as prime minister, those
some people very much including Curzon himself, who was
mortified when Baldwin was summoned to the Palace
instead.

After the embarrassment of Sir Alec Douglas-Home, the
Tories had decided to follow Labour's example and choose
their leaders by the only proper way in a Parliamentary
democracy: election by the party's MPs, who had themselves
been elected by millions of voters. In 1965 Edward Heath was
chosen that way, in 1975 Margaret Thatcher deposed him by

the same means. And in 1990 she herself was deposed by her MPs. After the Tories were routed in 1997, their next party conference saw MPs denounced and derided by speakers, none as contemptuous as Lord Archer of Weston-super-Mare, as the popular novelist Jeffrey Archer had become, playing on the political stage for the last time before his conviction and imprisonment for perjury.

But the damage was done, and his intervention at that conference helped push the Tories towards a disastrous course. A half-baked system was devised by which the MPs voted on candidates among their own number until they had reduced them to a shortlist of two, who then went on to a final vote by party members across the country. This might have made sense of a kind half a century before with party membership at 2.8 million. But membership had fallen, slowly at first and then precipitously, so that by the time the choice of leader was handed to the members they numbered barely a quarter of a million. Shrill cries from the right demanded that more power should be given to the party and to the members. But what party, and what members? At all events, this change had a very great effect on the Tories over the next turbulent decades.

Just how dangerous or damaging this strange system could be was very soon demonstrated after the 2001 defeat and Hague's resignation. Kenneth Clarke led the subsequent voting among the MPs, but when he and Iain Duncan Smith were the two put forward to the party members, Clarke lost decisively, by 39.3 per cent to 60.7 per cent. (Giving the results as percentages conveniently allowed the Tories to conceal what the actual membership was, which is to say how far it had declined.) The rump of members was decidedly more elderly, southern, prosperous, and right wing than the mass of Tory voters, let alone the whole population. Duncan Smith might have been more popular among party members, but Clarke was much more popular with the voters.

No sooner had this new scheme for choosing a leader been put in motion than its unwisdom was demonstrated. Duncan Smith was such an obvious dud that he lasted for a little more than two years before he was removed in one more Parliamentary coup. Rather than risk someone else who was obviously not up to the job, the Tory MPs took it on themselves to replace him with Michael Howard, pre-emptively chosen *nem. con.* so that the party members had no say. Howard at least steadied the ranks and achieved a partial recovery at the 2005 election.

Call Me Dave

After defeat at the 2005 election, Howard announced that he would resign, but not until December. This was a clever manoeuvre intended to give David Cameron the best shot at winning the leadership race. So he did, sealing victory at the party conference with a fluent speech delivered without notes or prompter. This was considered an astonishing feat in itself, although once upon a time Cicero could speak for three or more hours without any written words in front of him. David Davis, a libertarian Tory, led in the first ballot of MPs but in the second Cameron won ninety votes to Davis's fifty-seven, before easily wining among party members.

When Churchill became prime minister, and then Tory leader, he had been an MP for forty years, and had served as home secretary, first lord of the admiralty and chancellor of the Exchequer. Thatcher had first stood unsuccessfully for Parliament twenty-five years before she won the party leadership, by when she had sat in Parliament for sixteen years and had held office as a junior minister and then cabinet minister. When Cameron became leader he had never held office and had been an MP for little more than four years, although his election as member for Witney in 2001 had at least allowed

him to vote for Blair's catastrophic Iraq war. His elevation
came almost exactly forty years since Douglas-Home had
resigned the party leadership, and the choice of another patrician Etonian and Oxonian seemed an unlikely step. After
experimenting with so many plebeian leaders, all but one of
them failures, the party was once again singing, 'Bow, bow,
ye lower middle classes!' Cameron's father was a stockbroker
and chairman of White's, the grandest of St James's Street
clubs. His wife, Samantha, was the daughter of a baronet and
the stepdaughter of a peer. Apart from smoking a certain
amount of dope, at school and with 'Sam's friends', as he later
admitted, at Oxford Cameron joined the notorious Bullingdon Club, generation by generation a gang of upper-class
bravos who dine in blue tailcoats and leave wreckage behind
them. In *Decline and Fall*, his first novel, Evelyn Waugh glee-
fully described 'the sound of the English county families
baying for broken glass' as the 'Bollinger Club' enjoyed themselves: 'They broke up Mr Austen's grand piano, and stamped
Lord Rending's cigars into his carpet, and smashed his china,
and tore up Mr Partridge's sheets, and threw the Matisse into
his lavatory.'

Although the new prime minister's generation hadn't been
quite as destructive, a photograph emerged of the 'Buller',
including Cameron and Boris Johnson, wearing their quaint
finery, and wearing as well the 'sneer of cold command'. Roy
Hattersley, a former deputy leader of the Labour Party, said
that the photograph was more damaging than anything else
that could be said against the Tories. It didn't help that
George Osborne, five years younger than Cameron, and his
future chancellor of the Exchequer, had also belonged to
the Bullingdon. Osborne went to St Paul's rather than Eton,

but on the other hand he was the heir to a baronetcy and a substantial family fortune. At any rate, Cameron evidently agreed with Hattersley, since he went to some length to suppress the incriminating snapshot.

This comeback of the upper class was a surprising turn of events, and Cameron was acutely self-conscious about his public appearance, making a not particularly convincing attempt to present himself as a simple soul. Unlike Blair, Cameron didn't try to modulate his voice to more chummy populist tones on television, but he resigned from White's, and gave up shooting, which he enjoyed. Cameron might have done better to shrug off the Bullingdon photograph with a laugh, and to say that he liked White's, and enjoyed shooting. If not 'Damn your insolence', he could have said that he was what he was and didn't intend to compete with the traditional Labour custom of 'lowlier than thou'.

Maybe more remarkable than fancy-dress clubs was the fact of Oxford itself. There have been seventeen British prime ministers since 1945, of whom an astonishing, or maybe preposterous, thirteen have been Oxonians. The last Cambridge man at Number 10 was Baldwin, eighty-six years ago. There are comparisons in other countries, the dominance in French politics, administration and business of products of the *grandes écoles*, École normale supérieure, École Polytechnique and Sciences Po, or in America the preponderance of Ivy League alumni: not long ago every member of the Supreme Court had been to Harvard or Yale as an undergraduate or Law School student.

But nothing quite matches that dark blue colouring of English public life, or its importance for this story, and it may be that the Oxford Union debating society casts an even longer shadow than the Bullingdon. In November 1985, when John-son was intriguing assiduously and deviously to become president of the Union, the gossip column in *Cherwell*, the Oxford student paper, described the way that 'Balliol's blond bombshell' had turned for the moment into 'our Old Etonian Leninist', ingratiating himself with potential supporters from Ruskin, the college founded for working-class and trade union students. On the same page, *Cherwell* introduced a likely lad from Aberdeen who had arrived in Oxford that term: 'Michael [Gove, for it was he] conceals his rabidly reactionary political views under a Jane Austen cleric-like exterior,' before adding, 'watch this space for stories of eventual corruption . . .'

More serious questions would be raised by Cameron's adult career. He had a brief interlude as a political aide, one of the earliest of what would be the ubiquitous breed of 'spads' or special advisers to politicians, working for Norman Lamont, the chancellor of the Exchequer in John Major's government. An almost more embarrassing photograph on 'Black Wednesday' in 1992 showed Lamont announcing British withdrawal from the European exchange rate mech-anism in the face of huge financial speculation against sterling. Lurking in the background is young 'Dave'.

Then Cameron moved on to spend several lucrative years as head of public relations at Carlton, a second-rate television company with a dubious reputation. This was hardly suitable training for a statesman, and there he acquired a reputation for less than absolute veracity. Jeff Randall, a business jour-nalist who worked for several Fleet Street papers and then the BBC, said that after his experience of dealing with Cameron, he wouldn't trust him with his daughter's pocket money.

In the years Cameron spent as leader of the Opposition, he was nevertheless the first Tory in years who could lay a glove on Blair as they faced one another in the Commons, and he went on to outplay Gordon Brown comprehensively after Brown succeeded Blair in 2007. But that time in opposition also saw a bewildering series of policy reversals. At one moment Cameron talked about 'hugging a hoodie' – newspaper shorthand for his saying that the public should have sympathy for juvenile criminals. At the next, he wanted to get tough on crime by building more prisons.

There was also his mystifying volte-face over whether or not tax policy should be used to encourage the traditional family. In the most risible episode of all, Cameron attempted to parade his environmental authenticity by cycling from his home to Parliament. The effect was spoiled when the television cameras picked up a car trailing behind him with his clean shirts. (He has at least managed to turn this into a joke against himself.)

On occasion he took a braver line. He told his compatriots that the age of automatic retirement should be raised, and that no one should expect subsidised council homes for life. And yet, his attempts at straight talk didn't always ring true. Too often they were marred by an ingratiating desire to please whichever audience Cameron happened to be addressing. He was a member of the Conservative Friends of Israel, speaking to whom he professed his undying love for the Jewish state. Then in Ankara he described Gaza as a 'prison camp'. On a visit to Bangalore, Cameron noted sternly that Pakistan could not 'look both ways' on terrorism. Shortly afterward, while entertaining the Pakistani president, Asif Ali Zardari, at Chequers, the prime minister's country residence, Cameron spoke warmly about the 'unbreakable relationship between Britain and Pakistan based on our mutual interests'. Dave seemed quite good at looking both ways himself.

Some of his misspeaking was richly comical. While visiting the United States and speaking on ABC News, he uttered the usual platitudes about the special relationship, but went further by saying that 'we were the junior partner in 1940'. He apologised to one elderly lady for 'denigrating his own country', but he still enraged the *Daily Mail*, for once with good reason. They were able to wheel out aged Spitfire pilots and 'Desert Rats' who had fought in the North African campaign, and who hadn't forgotten that in 1940 the United States was neither a senior partner nor any other kind in the war against Hitler but was conspicuously and lucratively neutral.

But Cameron made two worse mistakes. He told a private dinner of journalists, that he was the 'heir to Blair', and the phrase was soon public knowledge. This completely misread the national mood. Everyone could see the total eclipse of socialism by the end of the twentieth century, both in its Leninist form and the milk-and-water Labour version. Everywhere the forces of capital had prevailed. The Soviet Union had imploded, while Russia degenerated with alarming speed into a brutal corrupt kleptocracy. 'People's China' also developed an astonishingly vibrant capitalist economy, albeit under the rigid political control of the Communist Party, with an explosive revolution in technologically advanced industries.

In England there was no chance whatever of a return to the dogmatic Fabian managerialism which had long been really the strongest Labour tendency, animating the Attlee government and memorably expressed by Douglas Jay in the words 'the gentleman in Whitehall really does know better what is good for the people than the people know themselves'. Thatcherism had been as much as anything a rejection of that view. But Blair had not only accepted the economic principles of Thatcherism, he had gone further, to the point where during his ten years as prime minister many of us had moved to the left simply by standing still.

Even Blair's vaunted success as an election winner looks dubious on closer examination. Although Labour 'won' a third election in 2005 thanks to the electoral system, gaining 355 out of 650 seats, its popular vote of 9.5 million meant that Blair had lost 4 million votes since eight years earlier. At 35 per cent it was little more than a third of votes cast. With the turnout barely risen at 61 per cent, little more than one-fifth of the total electorate had voted Labour; and for the first time in British electoral history, those voting for the largest party were outnumbered by those who didn't vote at all.

Only months after Cameron had become Tory leader, Blair was forced at last to announce his departure the following year. This was because of the Middle East, although not as might be supposed in the form of Iraq. In May 2006 Israel responded as usual to an attack on Bismarck's principle *à corsaire, corsaire et demi*, or if someone hits you then hit back harder. A fierce punitive offensive was launched into Lebanon. Even in Israel most people were hoping that this assault could be stopped well before it did, but almost from the outset there was a worldwide demand for a ceasefire, supported by a large majority of British people. But not by Blair, who now took his fealty to an extreme.

One cabinet minister said later, 'It was Lebanon that did it. There were only three countries in the world that were against a ceasefire. Israel was one. The United States was another. And we were the third. People were nauseated.' Since neither that nor any other minister actually resigned in protest, that might not have been the only nauseating thing about the episode. Although any belief in Blair's good faith or elementary honesty should have disappeared by then, he still had a handful of admirers. Just before he departed in 2007 he was interviewed in the *Guardian* by an adoring Timothy Garton Ash: 'Tony Blair bounds into the garden of 10 Downing Street, looking as if he's ready for another 10 years there . . . The outgoing prime minister seems full of energy, mental vigour and that almost compulsive passion to convince which he shares with Nicolas Sarkozy.'

This was an unhappy comparison even at the time, let alone in hindsight after 'Sarko' was convicted of corruption by French courts. If not quite corrupt in the same sense, Blair did something no prime minister before him had ever done, when he left government and Parliament on the same day. He immediately signed up for millions of dollars as an 'adviser' to a Swiss finance company and to J. P. Morgan, the Wall Street bank almost synonymous with the highest realms of high finance.

Then the crash of 2007–08 demolished Brown's carefully constructed reputation for 'prudence', or mere competence. The crash was of course a global phenomenon, and in particular we had the Americans to thank for such brilliant financial innovations as sub-prime mortgages, which meant lending money to people who could never possibly repay it, and credit default swaps, an ingenious financial instrument which, when combined with the mortgages, was akin to selling someone a disease. But Brown played his own part, with what he called a 'light touch' on the financial jungle of the City. After the collapse he was asked what had happened to his promise that there would be 'no return to boom and bust'. He replied that he had only ever said there would be no return to Tory boom and bust, an answer which almost raised questions about his sanity. He also said things had been fine while he was chancellor, and the only problem was that the banks and hedge funds had been behaving recklessly, 'but I didn't know that.' That could only prompt any ordinary citizen to say that if the chancellor of the Exchequer didn't know what the wizards of finance were up to, how were the rest of us supposed to know?

A Keen Political Intellect

With the unpopularity of the Labour government in his favour, Cameron managed one calamitous unforced error. 'Over the past fortnight, Mr Cameron's share price has wobbled in the markets,' Matthew d'Ancona, a former editor of the *Sunday Telegraph*, wrote in that paper in July 2007, 'but it recovered strongly on Thursday as the party announced the hiring of Andy Coulson . . . This is an unalloyed coup for the Tories, as Mr Coulson is one of the most formidable journalists of his generation, combining a sharp tabloid eye with a keen political intellect.'

Who was this formidable journalist? Coulson had written the 'Bizarre' showbusiness column in the *Sun*, before he was appointed editor of the *News of the World* in 2000, both papers of course owned by Rupert Murdoch, the overmighty Australian media magnate who had acquired not only those tabloids but *The Times* and *Sunday Times* as well. A hundred years earlier a similar position was occupied by Alfred Harmsworth, who became Lord Northcliffe. Sir Robert Ensor is worth quoting, looking back from 1935. Northcliffe 'was not really a Conservative . . . he had no Disraelian feeling for the greatness of the country's past and continuity of her institutions . . . He saw events and policies in terms of the headlines which would sell his papers; he was ignorant of history, indifferent to English political tradition; and yet he exerted over the party which ought to have conserved it a masterful sway, which the Parliamentary leaders were at once too proud to confess and too weak to curb.'

This is a remarkably accurate description of the Tories' relationship with Murdoch in the early twentieth century. Cameron undoubtedly thought that Coulson would provide a link with Murdoch, of whom Cameron was so frightened, and Cameron also cultivated a friendship with Rebekah Brooks, who became editor of the *Sun*. In 2011 a great crisis engulfed the Murdoch press when the use of systematic telephone hacking, or intercepting messages on people's mobile phones, became clear. Murdoch himself appeared before a Parliamentary committee in what he claimed was 'the most humble day of my life'. Brooks was tried but acquitted, but Coulson – whom Cameron with even greater folly had brought into Downing Street – was convicted and imprisoned.

By 2009 there was a perceptible sense of weariness with and even revulsion from the shabby Labour regime, although revulsion went beyond any one party. That year saw an outrageous scandal, when the abuse of Parliamentary expenses was exposed. Under the Attlee government these scarcely existed. MPs enjoyed free postage and a very modest travel allowance, and it was supposed that while they would visit their constituencies from time to time, it need not necessarily be very often. As 'constituency business' began to take up more and more of MPs' time it was deplored by both Attlee and Churchill, who both rightly thought that a member of Parliament's business was in the chamber of the House, debating legislation and holding the ministry to account, although that was done far too rarely.

Gradually more and more allowances were added, particularly or ostensibly to provide an MP with a home in his or her constituency and to allow him or her more time to hold what were pretentiously called 'surgeries' and dealing with 'case work'. The day would come when most of an MP's time was spent on such matters, and it was no accident this coincided with the decay of local government. The questions MPs deal with in their constituencies – housing, policing, schools, hospitals public, transport, street lighting – were all certainly important, but important *local* matters that could and should be dealt with at the local level.

Although Tory MPs were far from alone in their unprincipled greed, with some of the most outrageous expenses claims made by Labour MPs such as the late Sir Gerald Kaufman, it was the Tory claims that caught the eye. One Tory MP claimed expenses for a duck house island on a pond in his garden, one more for 'moat cleaning'. After Blair gave his last speech in the Commons he was clapped by MPs on both sides of the House, against all Parliamentary convention. One Tory MP angrily urged her colleagues to stand and clap, and it was consoling when her Parliamentary career was ended not long after by her own part in the expenses scandal. With all this, Cameron could have staked out his position by rejecting the inheritance of Blair and Brown. Instead he claimed it, while George Osborne, his future chancellor of the Exchequer, spoke of Blair as 'the master'.

Brokeback Buddies

Given the exhaustion of the Brown government and discredit into which 'New Labour' had fallen, by 2010 the Tories might have expected to win the general election decisively. Thanks largely to the expenses scandal, forcing numerous MPs to quit in disgrace, and some to be prosecuted and imprisoned, the election saw the largest turnover of MPs in a generation. But this didn't benefit the Tories as much as they had hoped, and the electoral system played its conjuring tricks again. The Tories won 36 per cent of the vote, but only 307 seats, depriving them of an outright Parliamentary majority. What became known as a 'hung Parliament' perplexed the party leaders, although it had been anything but unusual at Westminster: for much of the nineteenth and early twentieth centuries, minority governments or coalitions had been the rule rather than exception.

A grotesque episode followed the election, when three Labour schemers, Alastair Campbell, Peter Mandelson, and Lord Adonis, tried desperately to hang on to power even though Labour had won only 258 seats, sixty-eight short of a majority. One might have expected this from the first two old lags – but Andrew Adonis, the Goody Two-Shoes of progressive politics! What was he doing in that *galère*? In reality there was no feasible Parliamentary majority led by Labour that could be cobbled together with the Liberal Democrats, the Scottish Nationalists, the Democratic Unionist Party, and the solitary Green, all with their utterly disparate positions.

'We've won the fucking election!' George Osborne said angrily while these intrigues were taking place, and he had a point, although it would have been truer to say that Labour had lost the election. With no more than 29 per cent of the popular vote, 6 percentage points behind the Tories, or more than two million votes fewer than them, it would have been simply insulting to the electorate and to the spirit of democracy if Labour had remained in office. Nothing could have illustrated more clearly the emptiness of New Labour. Devoid of principle and existing only for the purpose of holding power rather than anything more exalted, they had come to believe that they were entitled to permanent office, or at worst were determined, as Lloyd George would have said, to perish with their drawn salaries in their hands.

During the election debates Nick Clegg, the Lib Dem leader, had acquired an unlikely new popularity, although that was partly by way of contrast with the irredeemably wooden Brown and the excessively smooth Cameron. The Lib Dems increased their popular vote if not their seats, but the fifty-seven seats they had won provided a clear majority combined with the Tories. When Clegg parlayed with both sides he was accused of whorishness by one Labour politician and of treachery by a 'progressive' columnist, but that was wrong.

And yet it was not improper, or at any rate unusual, for a centre party to play off the two large parties against each other. Some of those who were most critical of Clegg were also advocates of electoral reform and proportional voting, and under such systems there is very often a jockeying for position after an election. In the circumstances Clegg was entitled to speak to both Cameron and Brown, but the only realistic outcomes were a Tory minority government enjoying passive if sometimes critical support from the Lib Dems or a coalition between them.

Having accepted a coalition deal, Clegg was reviled at the time, and it would have very sorry consequences for his party. But a case, albeit a little tenuous, could be made for him. That election year saw the publication of Blair's memoir *A Journey*, a frankly weird book, all too revealing about Blair's deranged solipsism and sense of personal destiny, in a manner which makes reading much of the book seem like being stuck in a pub with someone who not only wants to tell you his own story but tries to explain how the meaning of life can be understood in terms of the dimensions of the Great Pyramid.

But he does have one or two good phrases, as when he says that the Lib Dems' problem was that they always wanted to be critics rather than actors. However hard as it is to warm to Clegg at this distance, especially after he followed Blair's example by going on from politics to a very highly paid job, in his case at Facebook, it can still be said in his defence that when he agreed to form a coalition with Cameron he accepted the burden of power and with it the burden of responsibility. This also meant swallowing firm commitments, particularly not to raise university fees, which the Lib

Dems had made when they didn't believe that they would ever be in government and have to honour such promises.

At any rate, a deal was struck between Tories and Lib Dems, who could claim that together 59 per cent of the electorate had supported them. As Brown lugubriously announced his resignation, Cameron told his wife, Sam, to 'get her frock on', and they sped to Buckingham Palace, where Cameron became prime minister of the first coalition government since 1945. It leapt into action rather in the manner of 1931, slashing public spending and introducing a frenzied series of reforms, while Cameron tried to cut a dash at home and abroad.

Side by side, he and Clegg appeared to be very much at ease with one another, two superficially plausible men of similar age and education (Eton and Oxford, Westminster and Cambridge). Someone coined the phrase 'the Brokeback coalition', and those who'd seen that 'ludicrous tear-jerker' (in David Sexton's sharp phrase) and then saw 'Dave' and Nick walk into the rose garden at Downing Street side by side could see the joke, even if, as one Labour MP pointed out, *Brokeback Mountain* did not end happily.

A faint aura of suspicion still lingered around Cameron, which might have been why the electorate hadn't granted him an outright victory. He had enough detractors: Labour was naturally bitter, as were malcontents on both the Lib Dem left and the Tory right – and the latter had loud voices in the press. Peter Hitchens of the *Mail on Sunday* and Simon Heffer in the *Daily Telegraph* were witheringly hostile: 'Because Mr Cameron believes in nothing except remaining Prime Minister . . .' began one characteristic Heffer sentence. Partisan critics could be shrugged off, and the animosity of the crankier left and right might have helped Cameron. But even those who were more kindly disposed toward him sometimes wondered what, if anything, lurked beneath his surface charm.

Soon the main purpose of this coalition became clear. Just as the 'National' Coalition of 1931 had done, the Cameron–Clegg government took an axe to public spending. A detailed analysis would take too long, but a few figures give some indication of the severity. Since 2010 funding for health has been cut by 4.8 per cent in real terms, which meant incalculably greater problems for the National Health Service. The cut for education was 15 per cent, housing 21.2 per cent. The Home Office budget has been cut by 38.1 per cent, and the Justice Department by 50.8 per cent. Since the last of those is responsible for prisons, and since more and more people have been imprisoned every year, this could only mean that conditions in many British prisons are more squalid and horrible than ever.

Most parties in modern democracies make promises to improve public services while cutting taxes, or at least without raising them. Most people are aware, or should be, that vast sums of public money are wasted; but identifying this waste while devoting public money to those areas where it's needed is far from easy. As it happened, while the Cameron–Clegg government was defunding health and education, the monstrous wastes of public money inherited from the last years of the Labour government were staring them in the face. For all that Blair had presented himself as well-nigh a small-state conservative, and Brown had preached 'prudence', they were addicted to *grands projets*, which proved insatiable maws for money.

Two dated from 2009. That year the *Queen Elizabeth*, a new aircraft carrier, was laid down, and plans to build a high-speed railway between London, Birmingham, Manchester, and Leeds were drawn up. Both were totally unneeded. The Royal Navy's remarkable if not always glorious history had culminated gloriously enough in a war to defeat the Third Reich and fascism. But the admirals, like the Tories, had not come to terms with our reduced status after that victorious war. In the 1930s admirals yearned for battleships, whose day had gone, while showing less enthusiasm for aircraft carriers, which would play a crucial part in that war. In the 2000s they wanted aircraft carriers, by now status symbols which would be of little use in any conflict the British was likely to take part in. Furthermore in the case of the *Queen Elizabeth* and her sister ship, the *Prince of Wales*, there was no foreseeable utility at all, since there were no aircraft for them when they were launched.

But the cost of that particular folly, around £8 billion, was dwarfed by the entirely grotesque HS2 high-speed railway. After it had been dreamed up by Labour politicians, notably Adonis, it found its way into both parties' manifestoes in 2010, Labour promising 'a high-speed rail line, linking North and South', while the Tories 'a national high-speed rail network'. From such cosy consensus ensued one of the greatest disasters and scandals of the age. By 2018 the Tory government stopped to look and asked for a comparison, and found the average price of building high-speed railway tracks in Europe was about £32 million per kilometre. By then, the first phase of HS2 to Birmingham was costing more like £250 million per kilometre.

If there was one field where the coalition government might also have made a new start it was foreign policy, notably in the Middle East. In 2008 Barack Obama had defeated Hillary Clinton for the Democratic nomination, above all because of her support of the Iraq war, for which she had voted in the Senate, but which he had not supported. Having defeated John McCain in the presidential election, Obama most foolishly appointed Mrs Clinton secretary of state.

One might have thought that the Western powers had been chastened by the failures in Afghanistan and Iraq, but no, Mrs Clinton embarked on yet another intervention. In 2011 Libya, long ruled despotically by Muammar Gaddafi, was beset by internal conflict, and the Americans began bombing. Before long she would say gloatingly about Gaddafi, 'We came, we saw, he died.' That might be phrased more accurately: she came, she saw, Gaddafi was sodomised with a metal pole before being beaten to death, whereupon Libya disintegrated into bloody chaos to become one of the chief recruiting grounds for violent jihadists, and the main channel for the awful human traffic which would see so many migrants drown in the Mediterranean. Another triumph for liberal interventionism!

This had been one chance for Cameron to preach restraint, but all too predictably he joined in the disastrous venture. Two years later another Arab country erupted into civil war. Obama hesitated to intervene in Syria against the brutal Assad regime, and was later rebuked for making promises he hadn't kept. But in any case the 'specially related' United Kingdom was not at his side. Cameron prudently decided that the question should be put to the House of Commons, and on 29 August 2013, the Commons dramatically voted against military intervention in Syria, despite Michael Gove, the most prominent Anglo-neocon in the government, roaming the lobbies shouting abuse at his Tory colleagues who were doing something sensible for a change.

A visibly shaken Cameron didn't dispute the result. This affected American policy also, and Obama drew back from further adventures. Not that there was much sign that interventionist zealots, in Washington or Westminster, had learned their lesson, although it was lucidly spelled out by a senior American official. As Philip Gordon, formerly of the National Security Council, put it, 'In Iraq, the US intervened and occupied, and the result was a costly disaster. In Libya, the US intervened and did not occupy, and the result was a costly disaster. In Syria, the US neither intervened nor occupied, and the result is a costly disaster.'

Another sagacious American voice was Aaron David Miller, a former State Department official who had been engaged in what was forlornly called the Israeli–Palestinian 'peace process'. After leaving the service he published an excellent book about that conflict with the painfully apt title *The Much Too Promised Land*. As Miller said, the Americans were stuck in the Middle East, a region they couldn't fix but couldn't quit, and where the United States was 'not liked, not respected and not feared'. It seems baffling why any British prime minister might want to ally his country with another that could be so described. A sensible conclusion to be drawn is that the British should at best be a friendly critic of American policy rather than a servile subordinate, but that evidently eluded not only those like Gove but most other Tories as well.

A Device So Alien

During the existence of the Cameron–Clegg coalition, domestic politics were far from placid, as a succession of events made clear. The 2010s was indeed a decade of much voting: four general elections, two elections to the European Parliament, one referendum in Scotland and two national referendums. The Liberal Democrats' Holy Grail had always been electoral reform, a change from the 'Westminster' system, or election of a single member by a simple plurality in a discrete Parliamentary district. As Condorcet had pointed out as long ago as the late eighteenth century, such a system was bound to penalise third candidates or parties, and for years the Lib Dems had seen their numbers elected to Parliament in far fewer numbers than their national vote might seem to justify: at the 2010 election the Lib Dems had gained 23 per cent of the popular vote but only won fifty-seven seats, a little more than one in twelve of the whole. As a quid pro quo for entering the coalition Clegg was therefore offered a referendum on the alternative vote.

In 1945 Churchill wanted to continue with the wartime coalition government and proposed to Attlee, the Labour leader who was still his deputy prime minister, that this continuance should be put to the people in a referendum. Attlee replied with characteristic briskness that he could never 'consent to the introduction into our national life of a device so alien to all our traditions as the referendum, which has only too often been the instrument of Nazism and fascism'. And thirty years later he was echoed by another prime minister of historical importance. 'Lord Attlee was right,' Margaret Thatcher said. 'Referendums are the device of dictators and demagogues.'

That device was first introduced in the year that Thatcher spoke, in 1975 by Harold Wilson. The United Kingdom had belatedly joined what was then still the European Economic Community in 1973. Wilson returned to power in 1974 but his Labour Party was riven by this question between supporters and opponents of membership, and so Wilson decided to hold a referendum the following year as a purely tactical device to hold his party together. It passed easily and seemed to quieten debate. Then further referendums were held in 1979 on devolved government for Scotland and Wales. The Welsh clearly rejected this proposal while the Scots narrowly voted in favour, but did not satisfy the agreed threshold. Under the next Labour government, Scotland and Wales both voted in favour of devolution.

As referendums became more common, and those who wanted them bandied the phrase 'losers' consent', meaning that defeat and all its implications should be conceded, no one made a principled case against them. It's supposed to be bad form to bring Hitler into an argument, but he introduces himself into this question. That's why Attlee spoke of 'the instrument of Nazism and fascism' and Thatcher said that 'referendums are the device of dictators and dema-gogues'. After he took power, Hitler held and won four referendums in his new Reich, the outcomes predictable in a terror state. But in 1935 a referendum was held in the Saarland in south-west Germany, which had been detached from the country after the Great War to please the French, on whether to rejoin the Reich, by then notorious for Gestapo, concentration camps, persecution and obliteration of all parties but one, as well as trade unions. In what was universally regarded as a free and fair contest with a very high turnout, the people of Saarland overwhelmingly voted for union with the Third Reich. Should the losers – liberals, Social Democrats, Communists – have given their consent to what happened to them?

At any rate, a referendum was held in 2011, asking, 'At present, the UK uses the "first past the post" system to elect MPs to the House of Commons. Should the "alternative vote" system be used instead?' On a low turnout of 42 per cent, the proposal was decisively rejected by 68 to 32 per cent, leaving Clegg looking foolish and disconsolate. Then in 2014 the people of Scotland voted on the question 'Should Scotland be an independent country?' By contrast, there was an extremely high turnout of 84.6 per cent, and 'No' won by 55.3 to 44.7 per cent.

Labour politicians had joined the Tories and Liberal Democrats in the 'Better Together' campaign opposed to independence, and this was resentfully held against Labour by many Scottish voters. On the morrow of the vote, Cameron said that the question of whether Scottish MPs at Westminster should continue to vote on English policies needed to be discussed, which was also if not quite logically resented in Scotland. In any case, that question would soon be overshadowed by another.

'Europe, fatal topic of Mrs Thatcher's last term!' Alan Watkins wrote in *A Conservative Coup*, his 1991 book about the fall of Thatcher. That wasn't actually the case, in the sense that what finally doomed Thatcher was the 'Community charge', universally and correctly known as the poll tax. Her obstinacy in pushing ahead with this deplorably devised and deeply unpopular measure was the last straw for many MPs worried about holding their seats.

But, of course, Europe had loomed over the Tories for years if not generations. In the last years of the Second World War Churchill had been deaf to his colleagues who wanted to talk about what was to come after victory, whether it was Attlee and Bevin of Labour concerned with postwar reconstruction or the Tories Eden and Duff Cooper, who tried to impress on Churchill that England would have the leadership of postwar Europe for the taking. As it was, after the war Churchill admirably urged reconciliation between France and Germany, but as the new European enterprise began to take shape he said in a somewhat oracular phrase that 'we are with them but not of them', while he continued in his delusions about the 'special relationship' and strength and unity of the Commonwealth.

There has been a somewhat futile debate as to whether Great Britain could have joined in the enterprise earlier and helped shape it. As it turned out, it was one Tory prime minister, Macmillan, who attempted to join the European Economic Community or Common Market before he was thwarted in 1963 by Charles de Gaulle, who had never forgotten Churchill telling him in 1944 that he would always choose Roosevelt over the French leader. And it was another Tory prime minister, Heath, who successfully took the country into the EEC in 1973. This was confirmed by the 1975 referendum in which Margaret Thatcher campaigned on the Remain side wearing a fetching jumper patterned with the European flags.

During her years in office the question of Europe became more and more of an irritant, between her and the other European leaders, and between her and her colleagues. It lay behind her falling out with the most important of them, Michael Heseltine, Nigel Lawson, and Geoffrey Howe. Her successor in 1990 was John Major. Not long after Major entered Number 10 Enoch Powell came to lunch at the *Sunday Telegraph*, for which I then wrote, and when I asked him about our new prime minister, he said, 'I simply find myself asking, does he really exist?' He did, and he remained in office for seven years, somehow holding together his fractious party. But there was a prolonged backbench rebellion over ratification of the Maastricht treaty, which turned the European Community into the European Union and took further steps towards that 'ever closer union' that the Eurocracy dreamt of.

Looking back over sixty years it's possible to think that the two most sagacious European leaders were de Gaulle, with his '*non* to supranationalism' and Thatcher with her 'No, no, no' to Jacques Delors's plans for a United States of Europe. The attempt to create one is an answer without a question, which can only damage what has been achieved already, and the proper goal of a very close confederation of sovereign states cooperating for their general good.

We have seen that at the 1997 election nearly a million Tory votes were lost to two Europhobic parties, including the United Kingdom Independence Party, generally called Ukip. That party survived during the thirteen years of Labour government, despite intestine feuds and splits, and its vote at Parliamentary elections, though still tiny, crept up, from a third of one per cent in 1997 to 2.2 per cent in 2005 to 3.1 per cent in 2010, while they regularly and unsuccessfully ran candidates in by-elections. But something was going on, and Ukip had tapped into an important vein of sentiment. By a nice irony, Ukip did much better at elections to the European Parliament, which they didn't believe in, elected by proportional representation, which they disapproved of.

It slowly became clear that Ukip was an important political phenomenon, and Nigel Farage, its leader, who has never won election to Parliament despite trying seven times, and whose party has never had more than one MP, could have some claim to be the most influential British politician of his time. In May 2014 I went to look at this phenomenon for myself, visiting a Ukip rally in Bath, and meeting Farage for lunch. The rally was fascinating. After the warm-up speeches, a hush of expectation fell as Farage was awaited. The Forum in Bath is an Art Deco movie theatre now used mostly for concerts and evangelical services, and on the last Tuesday of April it had the air of a revivalist meeting. In the foyer, they were selling books, button badges and even tea towels, while inside a lively, if middle-aged, audience nearly filled the former cinema.

They had come to hear their loquacious, dynamic, bumptious, bibulous, irrepressible leader, who was touring the country ahead of the elections to the European Parliament that month. He had himself been a member of that body for fifteen years and was of course about to be re-elected. These European elections are politically curious. Taken very seriously by the European elites, they are ignored by most of the populaces of most European countries, with turnout under 10 per cent not unusual. But they offer an opportunity for voters to express their broader discontent, which was indeed what was about to happen in 2014: on a 35 per cent turnout, Ukip won more seats than any other party.

Maybe because he thought he was about to upset the political apple cart, Farage had a swagger in his step as he took the stage at the Forum to thunderous applause. He spoke easily, at some length, with no notes or prompter, relentlessly hammering away at his theme: the country threw away its independence and is now governed by the Eurocrats of Brussels, who have let in a flood of immigrants from Bulgaria and Romania. All would be well if the United Kingdom left the European Union. Outside, there was a knot of demonstrators as well as a BBC television truck. Two protesters held a banner that said (incorrectly as it happens), 'Nigel Farage is a banker' (presumably intended as rhyming slang for 'wanker'), and one woman had a small handwritten placard reading, 'They called Hitler charismatic too.'

In addition to an egg thrown at him as he was walking through Nottingham three days later, a deluge of criticism and scandal had recently washed over him and his party – from allegations of financial impropriety to a concerted campaign to brand Ukip as racist, an accusation that some of its own activists had done nothing to discourage. And all of it was laughed off by Farage with cheeky bravado. At his peroration in Bath, he said that he had received a letter from a ninety-two-year-old former bomber pilot: 'Nigel, you only start getting flak when you're near the target!' Farage told me later that when he started speaking at Ukip meetings, 'Half the audience would be wearing Bomber Command ties!' those brave old men no doubt thinking wistfully of the days when they could express their Euroscepticism more practically by incinerating the inhabitants of Hamburg and Dresden.

He liked to dish out the flak as well as take it. In February 2010, Farage gained a measure of international fame, or notoriety, when Herman Van Rompuy, a Belgian politician who was the newly appointed president of the European Union, visited Strasbourg to address the Parliament. Farage told Van Rompuy to his face that he was a man with 'the charisma of a damp rag' – those tea towels on sale at the Ukip meeting in Bath bore Van Rompuy's face and the words 'Genuine Belgian Damp Rag' – and that no one outside Belgium had ever heard of him. It left Van Rompuy in stunned silence and quickly became a YouTube classic.

Among those who silently cheered Farage's vulgar assault were plenty of Tory MPs at Westminster, the ill-named Eurosceptics after the noble word 'sceptic', expressing the spirit of Montaigne or Hume, had been appropriated by zealots. True Eurosceptics were those who approved of the European Union, and a British membership, in principle but were ready to criticise its many failings. At any rate, those Tories were openly rebellious and disloyal to David Cameron, and closer to Ukip in spirit than to their own leader. However well it might do in these European elections, Ukip was still not then certain to win any seats at the British general election. And because Labour and the Liberal Democrats were opposed to a referendum on European withdrawal, one would be held only if the Conservatives won an absolute majority at Westminster. That seemed unlikely in 2014, particularly if the Tories lost more votes to Ukip.

Although Ukip had Europe as its central obsession, its support stemmed from discontent with much broader social and cultural change: a fundamental disquiet with the rapidly shifting face of England. And although Farage delighted some and disgusted others, no one was quite sure what to make of him, or even knew for sure who he was. And so, in order to write about it for the *New York Times* I invited him to lunch. We met at Boisdale, a restaurant that he frequents not far from Victoria Station and which itself deserves critical deconstruction. Much tartan is spread about, but then 'the owner is the heir to the chief clanship' of the Macdonalds of Clanranald, Farage assured me.

Before he joined me at the table he had been talking over drinks to party colleagues on the smoking deck above. Indeed, when later I came to look at the bill carefully, I found that I'd paid for their drinks as well as lunch, no doubt by an oversight. After we had washed down our lunch with champagne and 'this excellent claret', as he politely called the wine I'd ordered, we repaired upstairs for another glass of wine and, in his case, several more cigarettes.

He went to Dulwich College in south London, a school with the distinction of having educated P. G. Wodehouse and Raymond Chandler. By his own account, Farage was a noisy and annoying boy, and a letter from his school days recently returned to haunt him. When he was chosen to be a prefect, one of his teachers wrote an objection to the boy's offensively right-wing opinions. 'Of course I said some ridiculous things,' Farage said with a grin and a shrug. 'Not necessarily racist things.' Grinning and shrugging is something he does often.

Even as a boy he was already absorbed by politics. Farage knew the man who ran the Conservative Party in his village, 'who'd come back from India in '47 and who believed in drinks at six o'clock in a truly remarkable way', Farage said with a tinge of admiration. 'You know – six or seven large Scotches before dinner!' But his real conversion came after a visit to his school by Sir Keith Joseph, who was Margaret Thatcher's advance guard, the proto-apostle of a revived free-market creed. Farage says he was 'so taken by Keith Joseph that I joined the Tory Party at fourteen'.

At school he supposed that he would go to university or join the army 'and then think about the City'. But then Margaret Thatcher was elected in 1979. Her government cut taxes, and by 1986 came the Big Bang, the deregulation that quickly transformed the financial sector, for better or worse. Farage heard about the 'bright young things' in the City who were 'living hard, doing terribly well' and working at a frenetic pace. 'I thought, Well, I've got to become one of them as quickly as possible.' So he did, joining the London Metal Exchange as a broker. Farage's book *Flying Free* is quite readable by the admittedly low standards of political memoirs. In it, he cheerfully describes his City years, not quite an English Wolf of Wall Street but a lad making money fast through a long day and drinking hard through a long night, marrying, chasing women, divorcing.

When Thatcher was deposed, Farage was appalled. 'The way it was done – and the people that did it,' he snorted. 'Chinless bloody nobodies who wouldn't have existed without her.' He was disgusted also by the Maastricht treaty and joined Ukip. It was then a small and surprisingly cerebral body whose leaders notably included Alan Sked, a historian who taught at the London School of Economics. Farage quickly fell out with some party members. He says himself, in those days, he not only said but also did some ridiculous things.

Then, on the day of the 2010 general election he was in a light aircraft towing a Ukip banner when it crashed. Farage was very lucky to survive, and he then turned the disaster into a career move. The title of his memoir *Flying Free* alludes to the crash, and the back cover features a photograph of the author emerging dazed from the wreckage. His resolution in continuing to lead the party after that calamity impressed many voters, who overlooked the antics of his party colleagues, as one embarrassing episode followed another. Ukip called itself 'the libertarian anti-racist party', and one speaker in Bath said, 'If you're a racist, leave now.' That sounded like protesting too much, especially when one Ukip member denounced 'the Zionist Jews' and another told a popular black entertainer that he should live in a 'black country'.

All that was no more than 'saying some silly things on Twitter after a few pints', Farage claimed, and anyway those were people of no account in the party. But that couldn't excuse the egregious Godfrey Bloom, a Ukip Euro MP. By way of denouncing overseas aid, Bloom asked why the British were giving money to 'Bongo-Bongo-land'. When rebuked, he first said that he had intended 'President Bongo of Gabon' (the Gabon president was Ali Bongo Ondimba) and then, on television, that a bongo was 'a white antelope that lives in the forest' (they are actually auburn with white stripes).

When William Buckley was helping to mould the modern American conservative movement more than a half-century ago, his first task, he later said, was to purge the nasty racists and anti-Semites. Farage wanted us to believe that he had done the same. He was eager to tell me that he was speaking the following evening at a meeting organised by the *Jewish Chronicle*, that he had spoken at mosques several times and that his activists now included a rabbi and a Muslim businessman. Was this enough?

Still Banging On

Although he had told the Tories to 'stop banging on about Europe' Cameron still attempted to placate the bangers-on. A weak man in any case, Cameron chose drastic courses to give an illusion of strength. In January 2013 he gave a speech at the London headquarters of Bloomberg, the huge financial software and media company. In that speech Cameron committed himself to renegotiating terms of British membership of the European Union, and then to holding a referendum on whether this country should remain a member.

He possibly had in mind that 1975 referendum by which Wilson had intended to hold together his party over the question of Europe, which he won easily. And Cameron would also have recalled Blair's ruse. In 2004 he announced out of the blue, and to the horror of his Europhile supporters, that a referendum was to be held on the newly propagated European Constitution. This was the result of a private deal Blair had cut with the relentlessly Europhobic Murdoch, in return for the continuing support of Murdoch's tabloid the *Sun* before the general election the following spring. After that election had coincided with referendums in which the

Dutch and the French rejected the Constitution, Blair told the Commons that now 'there is no point in having a referendum, because of the uncertainty it would produce', at which he was reminded by the Tory MP Angela Browning of what he had told the *Sun* only weeks before: 'Even if the French voted no, we would have a referendum. That is a government promise.'

Quite lacking Wilson's sinuous guile or Blair's shamelessness, Cameron set a trap and then walked into it himself. He may have thought that he could avoid keeping his promise like Blair, or that he could pull off a victory like Wilson. The easiest way to achieve the first was to hope that the Tories would not win an outright majority at the general election in 2015 but would continue to govern in coalition with the ardently Europhile Lib Dems. As it was, the election upset many calculations, and for reasons that still aren't generally recognised.

Although the call for independence in Scotland had been easily defeated in the referendum, its aftermath had more than one consequence. It was at least a hypothetical possibility that one coalition would be replaced by another – Labour and the Scottish Nationalist Party. This might not in reality have been very likely, but the perception had a drastic effect. During the 2015 election campaign John Harris, whose 'Anywhere but Westminster' columns and webcasts had been one of the best things in the *Guardian*, or any paper, toured the country. With a week to go before polling, Harris reported from Nuneaton ('home town of George "Middlemarch" Eliot,' the *Guardian* helpfully explained), a seat that Labour had to win if they were going to gain a majority. There he found one message:

The Scots are always getting one over on the English, and some climactic Caledonian heist is now a very real prospect. Throughout the day, the same refrains repeatedly come back from people we meet: 'They wanted self-rule for their country, now they want to poke their bloody noses in ours . . . Nicola Sturgeon's after as much money as possible for Scotland, and I think they have a pretty good deal already . . . If the Scottish get with Labour, we're done for.'

On the eve of the election, a television crew from Channel 4 News was in Carlisle, in the far northwest of England, hard by Hadrian's Wall. They found just the same as Harris had. Two people stopped in the street both said that they had voted Labour all their lives but were voting Tory this time, because they were frightened of the 'Scot Nats'.

Even then, Tories and Labour appeared to be neck and neck as polling day on 7 May approached, with the lead regularly alternating: only ten days before election day a headline in the *Financial Times* read 'Poll gives Labour a 3-point lead,' and hopes were high at the headquarters of Ed Miliband, the Labour leader. On election day the polling stations close at 10 p.m. Just as Big Ben struck his chimes came the news from the exit polls. Cameron and the Tories were well ahead of Labour and on their way to a clear victory. Several people in the television studio expressed incredulity. Paddy Ashdown, the former Liberal Democrat leader, said that he would eat his hat if these figures were true, while a well-known pollster writhed with embarrassment as he wondered whether the exit polls could be accurate.

As the night wore on, they proved more than that, and every previous poll turned out to be wrong. At 1:30 a.m. the Tories held Nuneaton, having doubled their majority, and the game was up for Labour. There was worse to come. Had he won, Miliband would have made Ed Balls his chancellor of the Exchequer and Douglas Alexander his foreign secretary. At 8:30 on Friday morning the news that Balls had lost his seat in Yorkshire was greeted by raucous cheers on the trading floor of Credit Suisse, and no doubt other London banks as well. And then Alexander lost his seat near Glasgow to the SNP candidate, Mhairi Black, a twenty-year-old student who had not yet completed her degree. By the time the last votes were counted, that '3-point lead' over the Tories, if it ever existed, had turned into a 6.5-point lead for the Conservatives, who had 36.9 per cent of the popular vote to Labour's 30.4, and with 331 seats to Labour's 232 the Tories had an outright majority.

More startling than that, although Ukip had won only a solitary seat, they had gained an astonishing 12.6 per cent of the popular vote. It had long been assumed that Ukip was a repository for disaffected, reactionary middle-class Tories, but it had now cut heavily into the Labour vote as well by appealing to another disaffected group, the white working class. In the Yorkshire steel town of Sheffield, Labour managed to hold four of the five seats; and in three of those four, Ukip ran second.

Now Cameron was impaled, with no way of avoiding a referendum. It proved to be a dispiriting affair. As a Remainer myself, I can't claim that Remainers were 'the best' or Leavers 'the worst', but the rest of Yeats's line applied all too accurately: the Remainers lacked all conviction, while the

Leavers were full of passionate intensity. In *For the Record*, his excessively long memoir, Cameron takes us over the drama, but a reader might think his book the work of a Europhobic Brexiteer, so few good words does he have to say about the EU: 'Integration had gone too far,' he lamented. 'Brussels was too bureaucratic. Britain needed greater protections.' He complained that 'we had no hard-and-fast control over immigration as long as we were in the European Union'. And he deplored 'yet another treaty that reduced national vetoes and centralised power in Brussels'.

At the same time, 'I believed', he said fatuously, 'that in the long term, Turkey ought to be in the European Union', a belief for which he gives no convincing reason. In reality, there is and was no serious prospect whatever of Turkey joining the EU, now or 'in the long term', but by saying that, Cameron opened a space for the Leave campaign to claim in demagogic and xenophobic fashion that hordes of Turkish immigrants would soon descend on England's green and pleasant land. Altogether, Cameron's leadership of the Remain side was simply feeble.

During the campaign the name of Churchill was invoked with predictable frequency. Leavers called up the Dunkirk spirit, while the Duke of Wellington and Sir Nicholas Soames, Churchill's grandson, claimed that their illustrious forbears, Marlborough, the Iron Duke, and Sir Winston, would have supported Remain. Shortly before the vote, Cameron was asked whether he was a 'twenty-first-century Neville Chamberlain'. That was 'exactly the red rag needed to bring out my bullishness', he tells us, and so he replied, 'In my office I sit two yards away from the Cabinet Room where Winston Churchill decided in May 1940 to fight on against Hitler . . . he didn't want to be alone . . . but he didn't quit. He didn't quit on Europe . . . he didn't quit on European freedom. We want to fight for these things today.' Cameron called this his 'finest hour of the campaign'.

Like Blair's gruesome memoir, Cameron's was one more apology that didn't apologise. Just as Blair was sorry that things didn't quite work out as planned in Iraq, but not that he took us into the wretched war in the first place, so Cameron was sorry that he lost the Brexit referendum, but not that he called it. He says over and again, most unconvincingly, that he doesn't regret holding it. He insists just as often that he didn't promise a referendum to assuage the rabid right of his party or Ukip, and that he didn't assume he would win. But he is at his most absurd in claiming that a referendum was the only way of clearing the air and uniting the country.

Not only did the referendum divide the country more bitterly than any episode for a long time, with friends and families falling out, so far from bringing together the Tories as Wilson had seemed to bring together Labour in 1975, the Tories were torn apart. Some of the most prominent members of Cameron's cabinet campaigned for Leave. One was Michael Gove, he who had concealed the 'rabidly reactionary political views' noted when he was an undergraduate beneath an austere manner. He had worked for some years as a journalist at *The Times*, where he memorably wrote just as the Iraq war approached that 'Tony Blair is proving an outstanding Prime Minister . . . as a right-wing polemicist, all I can say looking at Mr Blair now is, what's not to like?' A good question indeed.

He was elected to Parliament in 2005 for a Surrey seat, since like other Scotch Tories he was unable to win a seat in his own country, and served as a cabinet minister in several posts after 2010. Then in 2016 he solemnly announced that he would support Leave, and defended this decision in a long and elaborate document that seemed to impress some more simple-minded folk although not everyone. One of John Le Carré's characters is described as 'a barmaid's idea of a gentleman'. Michael Gove was the Conservative Party's idea of an intellectual.

Blond Ambition

So then what was Boris Johnson? In the twenty years since he first wrote his fantastical dispatches from Brussels, he had become not only a public figure but one of the best-known people in the country. In 1999 he was appointed editor of the *Spectator*, promising its proprietor, Conrad Black, that he would give up the position if he were elected to Parliament. He was elected member for Henley in 2001, and was therefore able to vote for the Iraq war, but he hung on to his editorship for four more years. In 2008 he was elected mayor of London, defeating the far from universally popular Labour left-winger Ken Livingstone, briefly combining that post with his Parliamentary seat. And he was then re-elected, before returning to Parliament in 2015, although again he managed to combine that with remaining mayor for a year.

And he combined all these positions with another, as a celebrity or television personality. In 2009, when he was mayor of London, he made a guest appearance in *East-Enders,* the long-running television soap, looking in on 'the Vic', the Queen Victoria pub where so much of the action is set, grinning boyishly while he supped a pint while Peggy Mitchell, the pub landlady played by Barbara Windsor, simpered, 'I do so admire a man who dedicates his entire life to serving society.' Very few politicians get that kind of free exposure, and there was more to come with the 2012 London Olympics. Altogether F. R. Leavis's sharp phrase about the Sitwell siblings might have been borrowed: Johnson's career was an episode in the history of publicity rather than politics.

Despite heckling the Brussels Eurocrats, Johnson had never seriously suggested British departure from the European Union. In 2014, Anne Applebaum, the American neoconservative journalist, was visiting London and had dinner with Johnson, for whom she had worked at the *Spectator* some years earlier, and who now told her that no one sane would ever contemplate British departure. Two years later as the referendum approached, Johnson notoriously wrote two columns, one arguing for Remain and one for Leave, before deciding to publish the latter. A Tory politician with more nerve than sense of irony would say that this had been a 'Hegelian exercise', pitching thesis against antithesis.

There's a simpler way of putting it. Dominic Lawson has been another very prominent Conservative journalist, son of one of Mrs Thatcher's chancellors of the Exchequer, Nigel Lawson, and brother of the television chef Nigella Lawson. He had also been editor of the *Spectator* and then of the *Sunday Telegraph*, and had been a consistent critic of the European Union. And Lawson spelled out the truth, which is in its way the central fact of recent British politics: 'Boris Johnson was never in favour of Brexit, until he found it necessary to further his ambition to become Conservative leader.'

But there was more to it, and worse. Sarah Vine is another journalist, who was then married to Gove. She has related how, in the early morning after the referendum, she said to him, 'You're only supposed to blow the bloody doors off.' This is a much-quoted line from the 1969 caper movie *The Italian Job*. Michael Caine and an inept fellow villain are trying out explosives on a van in the middle of a field. After the vehicle is blown to pieces, Caine turns, and speaks those words. By relating that droll anecdote, Vine can only intend that Gove's intervention was a stratagem to further his own position in the Conservative Party, and that, when he backed Leave, he didn't expect them to win.

Nor, it is quite certain, did Johnson. He too thought that Remain would win, but that his support for Leave would hasten the moment when he became leader. Since it was widely reckoned that Johnson's intervention, along maybe with Gove's, helped tip the balance towards Leave, then the most consequential event of British politics in a generation was decided by the unprincipled personal ambition of two men.

Most prominent public figures divide opinion, but that can rarely have been so true as of Johnson. Millions of voters appeared susceptible to his appeal, but he was liked least by those who knew him best. Max Hastings, the editor of the *Daily Telegraph* for whom he worked, dismissed Johnson as a 'charlatan and sexual adventurer'. Matthew Parris, a former MP and aide to Thatcher, summarised Johnson's career, 'the casual dishonesty, the cruelty, the betrayal; and, beneath the betrayal, the emptiness of real ambition'. Ferdinand Mount, historian, novelist, former editor of the *Times Literary Supplement*, and another former adviser to Thatcher, for whom he wrote the 1983 Conservative election manifesto, called Johnson 'a seedy treacherous chancer'. Not a few Tories were to be reminded of that.

Immediately after the referendum Cameron announced his resignation, leaving the Tories to find a new leader who would succeed him as prime minister. The logic suggested that this should be someone who had supported Leave, most prominently Johnson. But there followed an exhilarating passage of infighting and betrayal. Gove might have been considered a candidate himself, but appeared to support Johnson, until a sudden change of heart when he announced that Johnson 'cannot provide the leadership or build the team for the task ahead'. As the *Daily Telegraph* said, this was 'the most spectacular political assassination in a generation'. Johnson withdrew, and so, after one round of voting among MPs, did every candidate apart from Theresa May, who became leader and prime minister by default.

She had been a Remainer, but now said that her task was to carry out the mandate of the British people, endlessly intoning an inane slogan. Visiting my old Oxford college in the autumn of 2017 I heard about an exam question. The Oxford syllabus 'Mods' and 'Greats' comprises a second part of philosophy and ancient history, preceded by Classical Moderations, which includes a logic paper. That year's Mods students were asked: '"Brexit means Brexit" – Examine this statement and what meaning, if any, it contains.' In practice, Brexit meant negotiating the terms for British withdrawal, which was far more difficult than had been foreseen.

When three judges ruled that the government could not ignore Parliament in these negotiations, the *Daily Mail* published photographs of the three on its front page beneath the headline 'Enemies of the People', the phrase which had been previously used by the Jacobins, the Bolsheviks, and the Third Reich before they disposed of such enemies. Although there were huge demonstrations by Remainers demanding a second referendum, that was never going to happen. Within a matter of years opinion polls were consistently showing a clear majority of British people, up to 58 per cent, who regretted Brexit and wished it could be undone, but it was too late.

For two years May struggled with negotiations, with a difficulty neither she nor any other Tory ever quite seemed to grasp. Malta is not the most important member state of the European Union, and Joseph Muscat was not the most esteemed head of government of those states even before his career ended in disgrace and scandal after the murder of an investigative journalist. But in January 2017, when he held the rotating presidency of the Union, Muscat was speaking for every other European government when he said something an intelligent ten-year-old could understand, if the Brexotics (as Ferdinand Mount called them) could not: 'We want a fair deal, but that fair deal needs to be inferior to membership.' That adumbrated the years ahead.

Inferior to Membership

For two years May struggled with negotiating British departure, but there were two stumbling blocks. In the Parliament elected in 2010, a large majority of MPs, including a clear majority of Tories, were in favour of remaining in the European Union. That was also true of the Parliaments elected in 2015 and 2017. After the referendum Parliament was thus supposed to carry out a policy which most of its members opposed, in a way which demonstrated the complete incompatibility of plebiscitary rule and Parliamentary government.

In 2002, when she was chairwoman of the Conservative Party, May had warned them that they were in danger of being seen as 'the nasty party', a pastoral rebuke from a vicar's daughter, though perhaps a misprision. No one had ever voted for the Tories because they were 'nice'. Their selling proposition against Labour was competence rather than amiability. In any case, when she was home secretary May had shown that she had a nasty streak herself, trying to demonstrate her toughness by boasting of a 'hostile environment' for illegal immigrants. Now she tried to impress the Brexotics on the benches behind her.

Maybe against her true nature, one might charitably suppose, May give the Brexotics the red meat of nationalism. 'Today,' she said, 'too many people in positions of power behave as though they have more in common with international elites than with the people down the road, the people they employ, the people they pass on the street . . . but if you believe you are a citizen of the world, you are a citizen of nowhere. You don't understand what citizenship means.' The xenophobic undertones of these words were audible enough even before a German historian compared them with another speech, about 'people who are at home both nowhere and everywhere, who do not have anywhere a soil on which they have grown up . . . and who feel at home everywhere'. That was Hitler in 1933.

When May had formed her new government in 2016 she began with some dramatic sackings, and settlings of score with both Leavers and Remainers. She told Gove to take some time off to learn the virtues of loyalty, although it was his disloyalty that had indirectly handed her the prime ministership. And she dismissed George Osborne, who had been chancellor of the Exchequer for six years. He had been a Remainer, while privately berating Cameron for holding 'your fucking referendum'. Not that leaving office seemed to cause Osborne much distress. He remained in Parliament for less than a year, and in February 2017, only eight months after leaving the Treasury, he found a nice little earner, as a part-time adviser to BlackRock, the largest fund manager in the world, which was happy to pay him £650,000 a year for working one day a week.

Gradually it became clear that the 2015 election victory was something of a poisoned chalice for any Tory prime minister. For Cameron it had meant that he had been obliged to call the referendum, which ended his career. And yet although the Tories had won an outright majority at that election, it was very slender, 330 seats, or just four more than the number needed for an outright Parliamentary majority. As other prime ministers have learned, small majorities hand exaggerated power to refractory backbenchers.

That was why Wilson, with a majority of just one seat over all other parties after the 1964 election, called another in 1966 to increase his majority. He did the same again in the course of one year in 1974. In the February election, he had only four more seats than the Tories and was short of an outright majority. He called another election in October which gave him, just as ten years before, an overall majority of one seat. Over the next five years, the Labour majority evaporated, and Callaghan, Wilson's successor, was obliged to strike deals with other parties, notably the Ulster Unionists; a foretaste of things to come.

Less than a year after she had formed her government May called another election in June 2017, hoping to increase her majority. Instead, she lost it, falling to 317 seats. To many people, the surprise of that election was the success of Labour led by Jeremy Corbyn. He had been elected to Parliament in 1983, the same year as Blair and Brown, but had been a permanent rebel ever since, espousing causes which meant much to a small group on the sectarian left but little to the electorate. He became leader by sheer accident. After Ed Miliband resigned, several candidates obtained the necessary support from fellow MPs. At the very last moment, Corbyn secured enough signatures, some of them from people who signed lightheartedly, never expecting him to be a serious runner, and were later horrified by the outcome.

When that election for leader began, Corbyn was 100 to 1 with bookmakers. But Miliband, in an attempt to widen the party membership, had opened it, together with the immediate right to vote for the leader, to anyone who paid less than the price of a pint of beer. In the summer of 2015, there was a craze among young people for Corbyn, which I witnessed from my own domestic focus group. Having won the leadership to widespread astonishment, maybe including his own, Corbyn was greeted by crowds at the Glastonbury music festival inanely chanting, 'Ooh, Jeremy Corbyn', and the craze lasted until the 2017 election. Or did it? There was another explanation for the greatly increased Labour vote from 9.3 to 12.8 million votes. The Brexotics claimed that the referendum was an emphatic victory which all must accept, but 16 million people, or more than 48 per cent, had after all voted Remain. They weren't likely to vote for a Tory party now ardently committed to Brexit.

Facing Parliament without a majority, May took a fateful step by enlisting the support of the Democratic Unionist Party from Ulster. The existence of this party was a signal reflection on the failure of successive British governments in Northern Ireland. After the violence erupted in the late 1960s, and the Provisional IRA began a campaign of terrorist violence, the initial response was to send in the army to perform a task for which it was entirely unsuited. Hence the calamitous and disgraceful episode in Londonderry in January 1972 when the soldiers of the Parachute Regiment opened fire and shot dead fourteen unarmed demonstrators. It slowly became clear that 'defeating the men of violence' in military terms was impossible, and so the next stage was to 'marginalise the men of violence'.

That meant encouraging the supposedly moderate parties: the Ulster Unionist Party, with whom Callaghan had struck his deal, and, on the nationalist side, the Social Democratic and Labour Party led by John Hume. Vast sums were poured into the province, which ended as something like the last Leninist political economy in Europe, with public spending a huge proportion of the total. A peace process was preceded by a 'pan-nationalist consensus', embracing the Dublin government, Hume's SDLP, Sinn Fein, and, in effect, the IRA.

In 1998 an agreement was reached in Belfast, which heard Blair say, 'A day like today is not a day for soundbites, really. But I feel the hand of history upon our shoulders.' The consequence was that the parties which London had tried to succour were eclipsed. David Trimble, the leader of the Ulster Unionists, was betrayed in a way that was very much a feature of Blair's career, his habit of giving an interlocutor to understand something, which Blair than quite forgot, leaving that interlocutor stranded, as had happened to Roy Jenkins and Paddy Ashdown before Trimble.

As for the other side, the peace process and the Belfast agreement had another outcome, which made a nonsense of thirty years of British policy. Seeing Hume side by side with Gerry Adams, chairman of Sinn Fein, and a former leader of the IRA, Catholic nationalist voters in Northern Ireland understandably enough thought, as Aneurin Bevan might have put it, why vote for the monkey when you can vote for the organ grinder? As one cynic in Belfast put it, Hume's final achievement had been to turn the SDLP into 'the political wing of Sinn Fein'. The SDLP withered away and was replaced by Sinn Fein as the largest nationalist party, while Trimble's official Unionists were overtaken by the zealous Democratic Unionist Party, whose most prominent figure was the hot-gospelling demagogic bigot Ian Paisley, and which had been accurately described by Enoch Powell as 'protestant Sinn Fein'.

In the fullness of time Paisley was to be seen side-by-side with Martin McGuinness, the former leader of the IRA, appearing to chuckle together, while Sinn Fein and the DUP formed an unlikely coalition which never looked as though it would last very long. And yet the DUP were the people to whom May now turned, desperate for the Parliamentary support. There were echoes not only of Callaghan's deal with the Unionists thirty years before but of Andrew Bonar Law and his 'Blenheim pledge' during the Ulster Crisis of 1912. As the crisis worsened, Bonar Law, leader of the party which supposedly stood for the constitution and the rule of law, came close to inciting civil war, and closer to urging mutiny in the army. The historian Sir Robert Ensor, who had lived through the Ulster crisis as a radical journalist, said a quarter-century later that this Blenheim pledge was a complete abandonment of responsibility by Bonar Law: 'It is difficult to imagine a Disraeli or a Peel, a Salisbury or a Balfour, so abdicating control. To pledge a great English party to follow a small Irish faction wherever it might lead would hardly have appealed to any of them.' May could have read those words with profit.

After purging some former colleagues, May made her most eye-catching appointment, of Johnson as foreign secretary. The reaction of much of the world was summed up by Carl Bildt, the former Swedish prime minister: 'I wish it was a joke.' In a way, it was just that, and it was certainly an embarrassment. Johnson went from one gaffe or blunder to another. He wrongly told a Commons committee that Nazanin Zaghari-Ratcliffe, who held British as well as Iranian citizenship and had been imprisoned by the fanatical and murderous Iranian regime, had been helping to train journalists, which was untrue and disastrous, ensuring that she continued to be held in prison.

He said that Sirte, the Libyan city devastated by Mrs Clinton's intervention, could become an economic success like Dubai: 'All they have to do is clear the dead bodies away.' Visiting Myanmar he started quoting Kipling's 'Mandalay' in his heedless way, causing grave offence and acute embarrassment to the officials accompanying him. More ominously for the future, he visited Northern Ireland and said that Brexit would leave the Irish border 'absolutely unchanged', which could not possibly be true.

Meantime, the Brexit negotiations continued awkwardly for another year, until July 2018, when May gathered her ministers to decide on a strategy that they could all accept, at which Johnson resigned. 'The toad!' exclaimed Parris on television, with monosyllabic eloquence. David Davis also resigned from the cabinet, but he, in his idiosyncratic way, was a principled libertarian. The idea of Johnson doing something out of sincere principle was what logicians call a closed category, like a square circle.

On 4 December, the government was charged with having failed to lay before Parliament legal advice on the proposed Brexit deal, and by 311 to 293 votes found to be in contempt of Parliament, the first time this had ever happened. The majority combined the Opposition and the Tory Brexotics.

May won a vote of confidence among the Conservative MPs not very comfortably by 200 to 117, with unhappy echoes of Thatcher's Pyrrhic victory in the 1990 ballot.

In the New Year there was no better news for May. On 15 January 2019, her government was defeated in the House of Commons by a margin of 230 (202 in favour and 432 opposed) on a 'first meaningful vote' to endorse her Brexit deal. It was the largest majority against a British government in history and would normally have led to the prime minister's resignation. But she pressed on, and on 12 March was again defeated in the Commons on the 'second meaningful vote' by 149 votes. Even before the third vote, which she lost again, it was clear that she could not go on. In the dread phrase, she was 'in office, but not in power', with all authority draining away from her. By its end, her government had seen fifty-one ministerial resignations in the space of three years, twelve from the Cabinet, most of them directly related to Brexit. May had effectively announced her intention to quit, confirming on 24 May that she would resign as party leader on 7 June. At last Johnson's hour had come.

Four ballots among the MPs reduced the candidates to Johnson and Jeremy Hunt, a Remainer who had succeeded Johnson as foreign secretary and had consistently warned of the dangers of a no-deal Brexit, which would be 'incredibly challenging economically'. The result of the members' vote was a foregone conclusion, Johnson winning two to one. More precisely, that was 92,153 to 46,656, which was to say that Johnson had been imposed on the country by people whom Wembley Stadium could nearly contain, and that the votes cast in all, under 140,000, represented the membership of a political party which, less than seventy years earlier could claim 2.8 million members. At the point where it could decide the fate of the country, the party membership was one-twentieth of the size it had been in its heyday.

There ensued six of the most dramatic and the most shameful months in British political history. Johnson was faced with the same impasse as May, which was to say negotiating a deal with the European Union which Parliament might approve. He could gamble, he could bully, or he could break the law. In the event he did all three. Culminating in the general election he called in December – the third in less than five years – and won with a substantial majority. For a few weeks or even months, the Brexotics and Johnson were ecstatic, before things began to fall apart.

Earlier I compared Johnson with Disraeli, but maybe there is a more apt comparison. When the Tories decided to pull out of the coalition government led by David Lloyd George in October 1922, Stanley Baldwin had damned Lloyd George with words – 'A dynamic force is a very terrible thing; it may crush you, but it is not necessarily right' – that could apply to Johnson. 'His rule was dynamic and sordid at the same time,' A. J. P. Taylor wrote of 'LG'; 'he repaid loyalty with disloyalty', and, not least, he was 'the first prime minister . . . since the Duke of Grafton [in the 1760s] to live openly with his mistress'. That last referred to Frances Stevenson, Lloyd George's secretary and mistress, an old-fashioned word for which there is no exact substitute in this context. Lloyd George's wife lived at home in Wales while he lived with Frances in Downing Street. Johnson moved into Downing Street with Carrie Symonds, to whom he was not married.

Does this matter, or is it relevant? Is it fair to mention such things? There was nothing new about Conservative politicians who led irregular private lives. And yet, even those of us instinctively reluctant to judge others in censorious fashion might wonder whether the old feminist slogan applied. In Boris Johnson's case, the personal really was political. The habit of deception, which had inevitably grown upon him in his personal life, was reflected in his quite unusual indifference to truthfulness in political life.

His waywardness with truth was well known, his ruthlessness less so, except perhaps to some women, and men as well, who had had dealings with him. He was faced with the same conundrum as May: how to strike a deal with the EU which Parliament would approve. Johnson had promised not only to 'Get Brexit Done', but to do so by 31 October, within a hundred days of his entering Number 10. His ultimate threat, a nuclear option as it was called, was to leave without a deal.

And without Parliamentary democracy, he might well have added. The Labour MP Hilary Benn proposed a bill which made 'no deal' impossible, and said that the deadline should be extended until an equitable agreement could be reached. That would have meant Johnson's missing his campaign promise, and he was determined to crush the bill. When twenty-one Tory MPs voted for it, he immediately removed the whip from them, in effect expelling them from the party and preventing them from standing as Conservatives at the next election. His hit list was truly impressive. It included Kenneth Clarke, who had been an MP since 1970, had sat in Mrs Thatcher's cabinet, holding several senior posts, and had been an effective chancellor of the Exchequer in Major's government. Philip Hammond was another former chancellor, in his case only a few months before. Dominic Grieve had been attorney general. And Sir Nicholas Soames, apart from his own Parliamentary career, had a particular resonance as Churchill's grandson. In addition, and without being pushed, Jo Johnson, Boris's brother, resigned from the government, citing 'irreconcilable, personal and family differences'.

Now Johnson called for the country 'to be released from the subjection of a Parliament that has outlived its usefulness', which the political journalist and novelist Robert Harris called 'appallingly fascistic' words. But they worked. If nothing else, Johnson showed remarkable determination and a capacity for bluffing. He had bluffed his way through the Brexit referendum, he had bluffed his way to Downing Street. And he now bluffed again by defying Parliament. In fact, he closed it in almost Cromwellian fashion. The ludicrous figure of Jacob Rees-Mogg flew to Scotland to ask the Queen, who was sheltering at Balmoral, to approve a prorogation, not that the poor woman had any choice about doing what her prime minister told her to do, even if that prorogation was ruled unlawful the following month.

On 2 October, Johnson told the party conference that Brexit would happen by the end of the month 'come what may'. He certainly meant to have his way whatever the consequences. When told that the agreement he was likely to reach would have damaging effects for British business, Johnson replied, 'Fuck business' – and everyone else, he might have added. If he was bluffing with the European Union, which had insisted that there could be no further negotiations, it worked. Instead of calling his bluff Brussels folded, and more negotiations were held. The EU acted partly out of sheer exhaustion and exasperation with an impossible British government, which the Europeans might by now have understandably wanted to see no more of.

During the referendum campaign the question of Northern Ireland had been far too little discussed. It should have been obvious that if the United Kingdom of Great Britain and Northern Ireland left the European Union, then the border between Northern Ireland and the Irish Republic, often contentious enough before then, would become the external perimeter of the EU. In the referendum, Northern Ireland voted clearly to Remain, with Catholic nationalists overwhelmingly supporting continued membership and some Protestant unionists doing so as well, although the DUP, with which May foolishly allied herself, supported Leave.

And yet, however fraught the politics of Northern Ireland remained even after the supposed settlement, nobody of any kind or on any side wanted a hard border between the two parts of the island. On the other hand, if the United Kingdom left the single market and customs union as well as the institutional EU, and the Irish border remained open, then there would have to be a different customs barrier, in the Irish Sea, and in a crucial respect, Northern Ireland and Great Britain would no longer be United.

A curiously named 'backstop' had been part of the previous deal enabling Northern Ireland to remain a fully integral part of the United Kingdom, but that in turn meant that the United Kingdom stayed in certain aspects within the EU single market. Now there was a deliberately ambiguous 'protocol', but behind a veil of words it did indeed

create a form of customs border between Northern Ireland
and Great Britain. In Ulster months earlier, Johnson had
insisted that this would never happen, but now, characteris-
tically following treachery with mendacity, he said that what
had happened had not happened.

'Dear Boris, Hallelujah!'

His final bluff was with Parliament itself, and again it worked. As part of the deal creating the coalition in 2010, a Fixed Term Parliament Act had been passed making it much more difficult for the prime minister to ask for a dissolution of Parliament and an election. Johnson needed enough MPs to support a dissolution. When the Liberal Democrats capitulated, he got it, and the Parliamentary stalemate of the past three years was broken. Any forlorn hopes of somehow reversing the result of the referendum were finished. The Brexit legislation was passed, and on 31 January 2020, after forty-seven years in Europe, the United Kingdom was set to leave the European Union. And an election was called for 12 December.

This time, Johnson was calculating that sheer exhaustion would lead many people to vote Tory just to get the wretched European business out of the way. He had one great advantage, in the form of the Labour leader. Although some ardent spirits had been delighted to find a Labour leader who was truly on the left, and for all the adolescent crooning of his name at Glastonbury, Corbyn had voted against EEC membership in 1975, opposed every European treaty since, and damned the single market as 'free trade dogma'.

Thoroughly middle class in origin, Corbyn was privately educated, and represented Islington North, which must contain more houses worth £1 million than all but two dozen other constituencies in the country. Although he had been an MP since 1983, few voters had any idea who he was when he became leader, but the more they learned about him the less they liked him. He had achieved an unforeseen success at the 2017 election for reasons already suggested, but then the spell broke, and that vote now looks like what the stock market calls a dead-cat bounce.

Polls had already shown Corbyn's extremely unfavourable personal ratings, even before most Labour candidates during this election reported the voters' sheer dislike of him. He had never had any serious contact at all with the industrial working class, as events now showed. Three years before, on the night the 'firewall' states Hillary Clinton had neglected because they were so obviously safe – Michigan, Pennsylvania, Wisconsin – fell to Donald Trump, one of her team exclaimed, 'What happened to our fucking firewall?' Labour supposed that its own 'red wall' in the working-class Midlands and North was safe forever, and in the early hours of 13 December, as seats held by Labour for more than seventy or eighty years fell to the Tories – Bolsover, Bassetlaw, Wakefield – someone at Labour headquarters very probably asked a similar baffled question. The Labour vote fell back to 32 per cent, with 202 seats the party now had its smallest number of MPs since 1935, and the Tories had won an outright majority of eighty, their largest majority since Thatcher more than three decades before.

For a moment it seemed possible that the Labour Party in its present form was finished. The right-wing press never ceased to howl about the terrible threat from Corbyn, but no effusion was weirder than one from Allister Heath, the editor of the *Sunday Telegraph*: 'Across the West, the forces of the extreme Left are on the march.' As anyone could see, across Europe the far left was everywhere in retreat, and the moderate left as well. If there was a spectre haunting Europe now, it was the spectre of 'populism', which might better be called demagogic nativism. Historic leftist parties – the French Socialists, the German Social Democrats, and others besides – reflected Labour's grave condition. Even allowing for that, Johnson seemed to have enjoyed a remarkable personal triumph.

Earlier it was said that Johnson divided opinion, and that phrase was more accurate than usual. With all the dislike and sheer contempt he inspired on one side, he was treated on the other with a hysterical adulation almost beyond anything Thatcher had enjoyed. A group of rich Brexotics threw a party to celebrate the election victory at an expensive Mayfair club, where Andrew Roberts, one of the hosts, the self-proclaimed 'extremely right-wing' provocateur and biographer, gave a speech that would, according to 'Taki' in the *Spectator*, 'have befitted Henry V after Agincourt'.

For much of the last century, the *Daily Telegraph* was a bastion of respectable suburban conservatism. It was grey, even dull, but also conspicuously honest. But now the *Telegraph* wasn't just a Johnson fanzine; it had a ring of the official journal of some third-world statelet or of a despotism worshipping the Great Helmsman or Dear Leader. 'It's time critics saw Boris for the Churchillian figure he is,' screeched Tim Stanley as he drooled over 'the blond magnificence'. 'Boris's win proves the soul of our nation is intact,' shrieked Allison Pearson. 'Dear Boris, Hallelujah!' shouted Roberts. Behind a fogeyish or stuffy exterior, no one was more ecstatically schoolgirlish than Charles Moore. Successively editor of the *Spectator*, *Sunday Telegraph*, and *Daily Telegraph*, author of the excellent three-volume official biography of Margaret Thatcher, he had some claim to be the most notable right-wing journalist of his age. He now wrote, in barely credible words, that Johnson 'is one of the very few people I have ever met who can be described as a genius', which suggested a sadly deprived range of acquaintance.

That comparison with Churchill was repetitiously made, along with endless invocations of 1940. Having acclaimed the Churchill biopic *Darkest Hour* as 'splendid Brexit propaganda', Moore would continue the comparison:

> Man, widely regarded by political colleagues as a charlatan, sees trouble coming from the European continent and risks his career on the point. His opponents are worried too, but see it as something which can be damped down. He is proved right. They are proved wrong. Respectable prime minister, who conscientiously got it wrong, cannot face the contest, leaves. Controversial, untrusted man who got it right leads, unites country, wins.

Grotesque as this conceit was, maybe there were comparisons with Churchill. In 1906, after he had bolted from the Tories to the Liberals and been rewarded with office, the High Tory *National Review* called Churchill 'the transatlantic type of demagogue ("Them's my sentiments and if they don't give satisfaction they can be changed") . . . It will be interesting to see how far a politician whom no one trusts will go in a country where character is supposed to count.' Three years later, Lord Knollys, private secretary to King Edward VII, said that, however Churchill's conduct might be explained, 'Of course it cannot be from conviction or principle. The very idea of his having either is enough to make one laugh.' And when in the early 1930s Churchill attached himself to the reactionary but sincere Tories who were fighting self-government for India, Lord Selborne, one of their number, said, 'He *discredits* us; *we* are acting from conviction but everybody knows Winston has no convictions; he has only joined us for what he can get out of it.'

Words like 'fascistic' don't really explain 'Boris'. If the only -ism Hollywood understands is plagiarism, as Dorothy Parker said, then the only -ism Johnson understands is opportunism. He had only taken up the cause of leaving the European Union to promote his personal ambition, which remained his motive over the next two years. The idea of Johnson having any conviction or principle is enough to make anyone laugh; he only joined Leave for what he could get out of it. And so the course of our history had been drastically altered by a man who had never genuinely believed anything apart from self-advancement and self-gratification. That is not a unique opinion. Max Hastings had said that 'scarcely anybody who knows him well trusts him', and one of the more repellent sights of 2019 was Tory MPs who to my knowledge didn't trust or respect Johnson at all nevertheless jumping on his bandwagon.

Wherein could Johnson's 'genius' be found? I have mentioned his journalism, which was notably repetitious: he wrote a column about his inability to resist going down and raiding the fridge at midnight for salami and cheese, and then wrote it again at least five times. It was true that he was often readable, and that he could make good jokes. While Blair was still prime minister he was enjoying, as he so often did, a luxurious holiday at someone else's expense, in this case in a castello in Tuscany with its own vineyard, olive groves, and farm producing delicious fare, the kind of place a north London literary foodie would kill to stay at. We had often wondered, Johnson wrote, what Blair was really for and against, but now we knew: 'He is *prosciutto* and *antipasto*.' Not bad at all, but scarcely the sign of statesmanship, or genius.

Or was that found in his books? His *Seventy-Two Virgins* can be skimmed for unintentional comedy, and in 2014 Johnson published *The Churchill Factor*, which became a bestseller. For Johnson, Churchill sometimes sounds 'like a chap who has had a few too many at a golf club bar', an enemy of his is an 'ocean-going creep', one of his friends is a 'carrot-topped Irish fantasist', Lord Halifax is 'the beanpole-shaped appeaser', one thing or another is 'wonky . . . bonkers . . . tootling'. This was the Finest Hour as related by Bertie Wooster.

In 1940 Churchill criticised a Foreign Office draft that erred 'in trying to be too clever' and was 'unsuited to the tragic simplicity and grandeur of the times and the issues at stake'. What might he have said about the 'genius' Johnson? But then maybe Johnson really is the man for our own age, an age incapable of tragic simplicity and grandeur. Orwell's

Newspeak was a language constructed so that it was strictly impossible to express any subversive sentiment. In Borispeak it's equally impossible to say anything serious, and he may indeed never have said, written, or thought a single serious thing in his life.

Plague Year

In 1991 Alan Watkins published *A Conservative Coup*, about the fall of Margaret Thatcher the previous autumn. By the time of his death in 2010, Watkins had been writing a weekly political column for the best part of fifty years, he knew Westminster intimately, and he interviewed many Tory MPs as he tried to unravel an event that had astonished the world. One of them was the affable John Biffen, who had served, somewhat unenthusiastically, in Thatcher's cabinet and who was quoted on the last page of the book: 'You know those maps on the Paris Metro that light up when you press a button to go from A to B? Well, it was like that. Someone pressed a button, and all the connections lit up.'

Those charming electric maps that illuminated the route from Sèvres-Lecourbe to the rue Saint-Maur have gone the way of the *petit bleu* and the *vespasienne*, and in any case no such figure of speech would do for the story of Thatcher's party since her departure, unless it were some kinetic construct, wildly flashing on and off at random.

After the turmoil of Brexit and the 2017 and 2019 elections, we began this story with Johnson riding high when the new year of 2020 began, 'dizzy with success', as Stalin might have said. He had seized the leadership of the Conservative Party and the prime ministership, thanks to his support three years earlier for a Brexit in which he had never believed. He had forced through a deal with the European Union even if he was obliged to misrepresent its character. He had prompted first a prorogation and then a dissolution of Parliament. He had won the election with the largest majority the Tories had known since Thatcher. And on 31 January he celebrated British departure from the European Union in triumphalist fashion.

Now more than ever he and other Tories liked to invoke memories of the last war. As it happened, two splendid nonagenarian Englishmen who knew that war at first-hand died in November, just before the election: Field Marshal Lord Bramall, a former head of the British army, and Sir Michael Howard, the great historian, Regius Professor of Modern History at Oxford, and professor at Yale. In another life, both had won the Military Cross leading infantry platoons, Bramall with the 60th Rifles in Belgium, Howard with the Coldstream Guards at Salerno. Both were committed Europeans and Remainers, and there was a bitter contrast between such men and the sabre-rattlers of the Europhobic right, whose bellicose sub-Churchillian rhetoric was always in inverse ratio to their experience of gunfire.

Not long after the referendum, I had had lunch in a Berkshire pub with Michael Howard and Mark James, his civil partner. Michael raised his glass with the words, 'To Hell with Brexit,' and he returned to the subject, as well as our new prime minister, when I last saw him in September 2019, physically frail but completely lucid. Max Hastings was a close and loyal friend of Howard's and was with him when he died, just after his ninety-seventh birthday. He has recorded one of the last things Howard said, about the 'extraordinary bathos' with which his long life was ending. His earliest memory was of the General Strike in 1926; he remembered the rise of Hitler; he was a schoolboy in 1940, a soldier two years later, before his illustrious career. And now his story was ending 'under the prime ministership of *Boris Johnson*' – spoken with awed contempt.

And yet not everything had gone quite as smoothly as Johnson might have hoped. One of the many false promises made both by the Leave campaign and by Johnson in the general election was that Brexit was to be followed by a glorious new age of free trade combined with trade agreements, above all with the United States. This was never likely in any case, and even less likely with Donald Trump in the White House. Other European parties of the nationalist right were, among other things, mostly critical of American power. By contrast, and to put it in the terms of the war they were always invoking, the Tories and the *Daily Telegraph* are *résistants* towards Brussels, but *pétainistes* towards Washington.

One of the Brexotics' favourite words of contempt was 'vassal' or 'vassalage' to describe our supposed subservience to the European Union, but they never stop talking about the 'special relationship', or nowadays the 'Anglosphere', with Roberts insisting that 'Britain will be better off as a junior partner of the United States than an EU vassal'. This is a tricky claim after we had seen what 'junior partnership' meant in practice. Whatever else Brussels may have done, British troops have never been sent to fight in criminal and catastrophic wars in the Middle East at the behest of Jacques

Delors or Jean-Claude Juncker. In fact, when Roberts says 'junior partner', he appears to mean 'vassal'.

Now Donald Trump presented a grave problem for the Anglospheroids, and for Johnson, who desperately needed Trump's goodwill in the hope of some trading arrangement, but knew that the president's very name was toxic in England. As the luck of the calendar had it, a NATO conference had taken place in London in the first week of December, days before the election, and it was most amusing to see the prime minister desperately avoiding any contact *à deux* with the president. In the New Year, weeks after the election, came Trump's assassination of Qassim Suleimani, the senior Iranian commander, and we could tell how important the 'special relationship' still was from the fact that Johnson was the very first leader Trump chose not to inform of his decision.

This crisis found Johnson sunning himself in the West Indies, and on his return, his government was at sixes and sevens. The secretary of state, Mike Pompeo, called on the foreign secretary, Dominic Raab, to repeat the president's demand that America's allies should renounce the Iran nuclear deal. Like a good vassal, Raab said that the government was 'looking very hard' at the deal, but almost simultaneously Johnson spoke to Hassan Rouhani, the Iranian president, to stress his support for it. Then on 14 January, Johnson turned around and said the earlier deal was 'flawed,' and so 'let's replace it with the Trump deal'. But really, did 'Brexit Britain' have any coherent foreign policy at all?

Still Johnson preened and boasted about the glories of Brexit and new freedoms. The influence of P. G. Wodehouse on his literary manner has already been mentioned, but he had forgotten what Bertie Wooster once observed: 'It's always just when a fellow is feeling particularly braced with things in general that Fate sneaks up behind him with a bit of lead piping.' Or again, as a classicist, Johnson presumably knew that hubris is followed by nemesis. In his case it took the form of Covid-19, which sneaked up behind him in February and March.

So grievous was the pandemic for the British people, and so bitter the lingering arguments about the correct response, that we still don't know for sure the full story. If life is lived forward but understood backward, as Kierkegaard said, then that applies with peculiar force to British politics in the past five years as we have tried to make sense of those events and pass judgement. The Covid inquiry in late 2023 was unsatisfactory for anyone hoping for a calm and attached analysis of how the pandemic was handled.

But one thing became clear, although it should have been ever since Johnson emerged into public view. He might have been a successful cheerleader or rabble-rouser or entertainer, but he was quite exceptionally ill-equipped to deal with a grave crisis. So far from 'omnium consensu capax imperii nisi imperasset', Tacitus' lapidary phrase about Galba – 'everyone would have agreed that he was worthy of the imperial office, if he had never held it' – no one who could see and hear and think straight and had followed Johnson's career would have supposed him worthy of the prime ministership, even before he gave a practical demonstration of his unworthiness in grim circumstances.

Having first boasted that he had been shaking hands with everyone he met, including Covid patients he had visited in

hospitals, and his initial shilly-shallying, which would indeed
characterise the next two years, a complete lockdown was
ordered. The entire populace was told to stay indoors. Johnson
appeared on television trying to look solemn and suppress
the smirk which was his default expression, to say that everyone must stay indoors. This instruction would take on a
gruesomely ironic resonance.

People did stay at home unless they contracted Covid
severely enough to be taken to hospital, where doctors,
nurses, and porters worked heroically. So did the scientists
who set out with extreme urgency to find a vaccine. Latter-
day critics of lockdown such as Lord Sumption – the very
highly paid commercial barrister, and distinguished historian, who become a judge of the Supreme Court, and then
after retiring from the bench a pundit with many strong
opinions – have suggested that it was quite unnecessary.
They said we should have followed the example of Sweden,
where the populace were merely told to observe sensible
precautions and allowed to carry on much as usual, and
where the fatality rate was no higher than Great Britain's.
But Sweden is so disparate from Great Britain – still largely
rural, with a population one-sixth, and a density of population one-tenth, of the British – that the comparison was
highly misleading.

We don't know what would have happened without lockdown; we do know what happened in any case. There were
about 24.8 million British cases of Covid (some people had
it more than once) and more than 231,000 deaths, an inci-
dence of fatality the country had not known since its last
great war in 1945. One of the first to fall gravely ill was
Johnson himself, who at the beginning of April was taken to

hospital and was soon in intensive care on oxygen, touch and go whether he would survive. He was in a high-risk category because he was so grossly overweight, a man of five-foot-nine weighing seventeen stone.

His illness occasioned an even more hysterical response from his worshippers at the *Daily Telegraph*, in particular Allison Pearson, whose column headed 'Only now do we realise how valuable Boris is to us all' began tremulously, 'How is Boris? For millions of people, that was our first thought upon waking yesterday. And our last thought before we fell asleep the night before. The prospect of losing our Prime Minister was profoundly shocking. "He won't die, will he?" a friend texted at 11.18 p.m. "My heart will break."' And Pearson continued:

> Boris is loved – really loved – in a way that the metropolitan media class has never begun to understand. Hearing reporters and doctors on TV talking about the PM's admission to the ICU at St Thomas's Hospital, discussing the likely effect on his lungs and 'other vital organs', was horrible; the picture of naked vulnerability it painted so entirely at odds with our rambunctious hero barrelling into a room with a quizzical rub of that blond mop and a booming: 'Hi, folks!' Yet, make no mistake, the health of Boris Johnson is the health of the body politic and, by extension, the health of the nation itself. All 66 million of us are metaphorically pacing the hospital corridor, desperate for news.

This drivel is worth quoting only to illustrate the way in which the pandemic was somehow a fitting climax to the febrile and unbalanced atmosphere of the previous few years.

There was another kind of hysterical screeching, inside 10 Downing Street. Dominic Cummings was the weird guru who was said to have masterminded the Leave campaign in the referendum. Johnson then took him on, and then made the same mistake that Blair had made with Alastair Campbell, bringing a venomous, unreliable hitman into the heart of government. If the second module of the 2023 Covid inquiry taught us nothing about how the pandemic might or should have been handled, we learned more than we wanted to know about the atmosphere inside Johnson's Downing Street, from Cummings's WhatsApp exchanges.

In August 2020, the prime minister's chief adviser wrote to Lee Cain, another of his team, about Helen MacNamara, the deputy cabinet secretary:

> If i have to come back to Helen's bullshit with PET [propriety and ethics team] designed to waste huge amounts of my time so i cant spend it on other stuff – I will personally handcuff her and escort her from the building. I dont care how it is done but that woman must be out of our hair – we cannot keep dealing with this horrific meltdown of the british state while dodging stilettos from that cunt.

Besides that, Cummings referred to cabinet ministers as 'feral' and 'useless fuckpigs', which to be fair was a reasonable if excessively colloquial description of several of them. Before long the strain was too much for some, such as Lord Geidt, who resigned from his position, even if that position, 'ethics adviser to Boris Johnson', was reminiscent of what Oliver St John Gogarty called the Royal Hibernian Academy, a treble contradiction in terms.

Above all we learned about Johnson himself, recovered from the virus, back at Downing Street, and careering about like a supermarket trolley, in the phrase his colleagues continually used. He was hopelessly indecisive, one day wondering whether they should let 'the bodies pile high in the street', next appearing on television to remind us to stay at home. It was not a personal opinion that these appearances were embarrassing and feeble: there was a point of comparison. In April, the Queen, now aged ninety-three, spoke on television. Quite apart from Johnson's fatuous book on Churchill, politicians continually try to invoke the Finest Hour, but in an address which impressed even committed republicans the Queen didn't need any rhetorical effect. She merely reminded the nation that she had first broadcast on the BBC as a fifteen-year-old girl in 1940. And she ended with another echo of a war towards whose end she had served as an army mechanic. 'We should take comfort that, while we may have more still to endure, better days will return: we will be with our friends again; we will be with our families again; we will meet again.'

In her dignity and simplicity the Queen provided an antithesis to her prime minister. Before Robert Harris became a political journalist and then novelist he had been president of the Cambridge Union. He remarked correctly that, every time he heard him, he was surprised again by what a very poor public speaker Johnson is. And he also said that whenever we heard those mock-solemn addresses from the prime minister, with their absurd excuses and totally

unconvincing explanations, we all knew what being married
to him must be like.

At length the vaccines were rolled out and we were all
jabbed. And then we learned about the parties. Almost
all citizens were carefully obeying the instructions to stay
indoors and not meet family and friends. People were unable
to visit their dying parents in hospital or, in one especially
poignant case, a mother was unable to visit her dying
sixteen-year-old son. Two elderly women sitting and talking
together on a bench on the Derbyshire hills were arrested
by an overzealous policeman. During all this, Downing
Street was one long bacchanal, with parties celebrating this
and that, 'Bring your own booze', suitcases full of bottles
being wheeled to the garden entrance of Number 10, a party
on the evening before Prince Philip's funeral, another
party for the prime minister's birthday.

One of his dwindling band of defenders said that Johnson
had not known about the gathering but had been 'ambushed
by a cake'; others said that these gatherings had not really
been parties, at which the excellent Bob Marshall-Andrews,
the former left-wing Labour MP, wrote to *The Times* to say
he had 'recently been offered a speed awareness course to
avoid the inevitable fine for my latest offence (26mph in a
20mph limit). Is there not a compelling case for a "party
awareness course" to help people to appreciate when they are
at a party?'

And the man who set the tone for all this staggered
on, unaware how fragile his position was. But the rest of
us should not have been surprised. At the height of the
Watergate imbroglio in the spring of 1974, two celebrated
American conservatives were talking: Barry Goldwater, the

unsuccessful republican candidate in 1964, and William Buckley the founder and editor of the *National Review*, journal of the new right. Goldwater said that if all of this had been described to him ten years before – the dirty tricks, the burglars and the bunglers, chaos in the Oval Office, and the administration paralysed – 'I'd have said, my, this must mean Dick Nixon is in the White House!' In the same way, if a few years earlier we had been told about another imbroglio, a chaotic, disintegrating government, with the prime minister's chief adviser calling a senior civil servant a 'cunt' and cabinet ministers 'stupid fuckpigs', with endless carousing at Downing Street while others obeyed the law, and a hopelessly indecisive man supposedly in charge, we might have said, 'Oh my God, you don't mean Boris Johnson is prime minister?'

'In the name of God, go'

However insubstantial Johnson was, and however insignificant his achievements may seem in the eye of history, he found time to do real damage, with a shameful raft of legislation in the spring of 2022: Ferdinand Mount compared this with the infamous Six Acts passed by the reactionary government of Lord Liverpool in 1819. The Nationality and Borders Act was presented as a measure to stop the traffic in illegal immigrants, while allowing the deportation of asylum-seekers to Rwanda, a detail which could not have been dreamed up by any satirist. Less cruel but more ominous, the Elections Act required voters for the first time in British history to produce identification. Impersonation had never at any time been anything remotely like a serious problem in Great Britain (although in parts of Ireland, as well as in Irish Boston, the old slogan 'vote early, vote often' had sometimes operated). This act was quite obviously a piece of voter suppression worthy of the American Republicans, intended to discourage poorer voters who would be less likely to carry photographic identification.

The Fixed-Term Parliament Act passed to bind together the Tories and Liberal Democrats had never been a good idea, patently weakening the power of Parliament to bring down governments. But the Dissolution and Calling of Parliament Act did more than just repeal that law. It ensured 'the non-justiciability of the revived prerogative powers', which is to say made impossible an intervention by the Supreme Court against the prime minister's abuse of his power, as had happened in 2019. The Judicial Review and Courts Act, Mount wrote, 'while claiming to uphold the right of individuals to obtain remedy against unjust treatment, in practice nibbles away at the individual's rights of appeal and access'. When he became prime minister Johnson had been working on a book on Shakespeare, to which he has returned, while the rest of us brooded upon Mark Antony's words: 'The evil that men do lives after them.'

When the end came for Johnson it had nothing to do with those disgraceful measures, or even with politics in the broader sense. It was a question of personal conduct, and it should not really have been any surprise. His fall might have been unforeseen, certainly by Johnson himself, but it was surely overdetermined. The Tories had always known what he was like and sensed that he was an accident waiting to happen, and his relationship with his MPs had always been transactional. He was useful to them as long as he was useful to them.

A significant part in the story was played by Charles Moore. In the final volume of his authorised life of Thatcher, *Herself Alone*, there is an account of her fall, written with barely restrained emotion by an author keenly attached to his subject. That's expressed by the book's epigraph, 'When lovely woman stoops to folly, / And finds too late that men betray . . .' (which well-known lines, in the sense that Oliver Goldsmith intended them, might seem to apply more aptly to the personal life of Boris Johnson than the political life of Margaret Thatcher), and then when the biographer writes with lachrymose grandiloquence about the 'tragic spectacle of a woman's greatness overborne by the littleness of men'.

But not even Moore, embarrassingly infatuated as he was with 'Boris', could write similar words about his eviction from Downing Street. If Thatcher's fall was tragic, then his was truly 'the second time as farce'. In one respect, Johnson decidedly set the tone for a contemporary Tory party that has been plagued by sexual and financial scandal. I have said that sexual impropriety among politicians is nothing new, or necessarily important. But what distinguishes the Tories nowadays is not marital infidelity or sexual variety so much as sheer squalor. One MP was imprisoned for sexual abuse of minors, another was forced to resign when a woman MP sitting in the chamber of the Commons noticed that he was looking at pornography on his mobile phone.

A score-settling description of Johnson's ineptitude during the pandemic was published by Matt Hancock. He was the health secretary until his own political career ended when a CCTV camera caught him in a passionate embrace in his ministerial office with a colleague who proved to be also his mistress, transgressing lockdown rules as well as the Seventh Commandment; this time history repeated as bedroom farce. Hancock later appeared on a grotesque 'reality programme' eating the genitals of exotic animals in the jungle, and he looked more and more like our present-day answer to the Rector of Stiffkey, who was defrocked in the 1930s for devoting excessive pastoral care to chorus girls and ended his days exhibiting himself in a barrel at a circus before, sad to say, he was eaten by a lion.

Months after Hancock's departure, in November 2021, a United Nations Climate Change Conference was held in Glasgow. The Tory right and its echo chamber in the press has long been contemptuous of what Moore called 'climate alarmists', insisting that all attempts to reduce carbon emissions were part of a left-wing conspiracy, and quite forgetting that the very first national leader to give a speech warning of the danger of global warming had been Margaret Thatcher. There was no point in lamenting the irony of a 'Conservative' Party which evidently had no wish to conserve the environment, and whose precept seemed to be Groucho Marx's 'What's posterity ever done for me?'

To give a practical demonstration of his view on carbon emission, Johnson flew to Glasgow and back in a private jet. In his opening address to the conference he appeared to take the subject seriously by way of evoking the end of a James Bond movie in which the hero is 'strapped to a doomsday device, desperately trying to work out which coloured wire to pull to turn it off, while a red digital clock ticks down remorselessly to a detonation'. He little guessed that a clock was ticking remorselessly down on his own position. He had shrugged off the joint report of two House of Commons all-party committees, describing his slow and muddled response to the beginnings of the pandemic in March 2020 as 'one of the most important public health failures the United Kingdom has ever experienced'. It would not be long before he could shrug off failure no longer.

His purpose in flying back to London was to attend a now-celebrated dinner at the Garrick Club in November 2021 for former colleagues at the *Daily Telegraph*, from which Johnson emerged talking to Moore. As one cabinet minister had said, 'The first rule of politics is that if you listen to Charles Moore and do the complete opposite of what he says, you won't go far wrong.' But Johnson forgot that when Moore urged him to help Moore's old friend Owen Paterson, an MP and former minister who was facing suspension for being paid to lobby ministers on behalf of outside interests. Anyone, voter or even MP, could see that Paterson had blatantly breached Parliamentary rules, and yet Johnson, who has spent his life breaking rules of every kind, tried to steamroller his MPs into bending their own rules on Paterson's behalf.

That was perhaps the antepenultimate straw on the camel's back. In January 2022, Johnson apologised to MPs in the Commons for 'attending an event in the Downing Street garden during the first lockdown', saying that he thought it was 'a work event', but suspicion mounted that he had, on that occasion and others, misled Parliament, which is even in these decayed times a grave offence. There was a further frisson over the lavish redecoration of the prime minister's flat in Downing Street, and although the details remained murky it seemed very likely that Johnson, whose ever casual attitude towards money and the proper conventions, had received sums from large Tory donors such as Lords Brownlow and Bamford, and that some of this money might have paid for redecoration.

Early in the new year, David Davis, the libertarian Tory, spoke in the Commons echoing Leo Amery in the 1940 debate that ended Neville Chamberlain's prime ministership, when Amery had in turn echoed Cromwell: 'You have sat there too long for all the good you have done. In the name of God, go.' As discontent mounted among the Conservative MPs, and the cabinet, the very last straw came when Chris Pincher, the deputy chief whip, was seen at a party at the Carlton Club, the Tories' historic unofficial headquarters, fondling the groins of younger men. When told about this, Johnson initially responded, with his ready wit, 'Pincher by name, pincher by nature.' What then happened was rather like the saying about how you go bankrupt, first slowly, then quickly. Murmurs of discontent became plans to gather letters calling for a vote of no confidence in Johnson. It was held on 6 June and, although Johnson won by 211 votes to 148, the game was up.

Very quickly the resignations began. On 5 July Rishi Sunak and Sajid Javid, the chancellor of the Exchequer and the health secretary, both resigned, precipitating a flood of resignations from the government, thirty-one by the following afternoon, when Starmer made by his standards quite a good joke, about the 'sinking ships leaving the rat.' Another was Gove, who told Johnson he ought to go, to which Johnson responded by sacking him. But it was no use. At 12:30 p.m. on 7 July Johnson announced his resignation, with the characteristic words, 'Hasta la vista, baby,' and both the pound sterling and the stock market rose sharply, little guessing what the autumn would bring.

After the Tory MPs had gone through the usual procedure and whittled down candidates to two, it was a mark of the party's fractious and dispirited condition that those two, Rishi Sunak and Liz Truss, were scarcely names to be conjured with, or even recognised, by most of the electorate. Mary Elizabeth Truss was then forty-seven, the daughter of parents 'to the left of Labour', as she said, and her father, an academic mathematician, had taken the family to live, if not for long, in what was still Communist Poland. As an undergraduate she was an active Liberal Democrat, before the Damascene conversion which turned her into what Keynes would have called a laissez-fairy.

Four years younger than her, Sunak was the son of humble immigrants, of Punjabi origin but east African by birth, children of the earlier Indian diaspora whose presence in Kenya and Uganda had been so much hated by Churchill as well as white settlers. They were the archetype of industrious, upwardly mobile immigrants, the father a doctor and the mother a pharmacist, who worked hard to send their son to a good prep school from which he won a scholarship to Winchester, the oldest of the famous English public schools.

Needless to say, both candidates went to Oxford, continuing that university's extraordinary dominance of British politics, and of course they both read PPE. A case has been made that this degree course – a dubious mishmash of politics, philosophy, and economics – has been the bane of English public life. It would take too long to list all the Oxford PPE graduates who have sat on either front bench over the past twenty years, from the years of the Cameron government, when the prime minister and the leader of the opposition, Ed Miliband, were both PPE people, until the time of writing when the chancellor and shadow chancellor, Jeremy Hunt and Rachel Reeves, are another two.

After spending a few years in business Truss was elected to Parliament in 2010, and as a reflection of the paucity of talent on the Tory benches she was shortly afterward appointed a junior minister and joined the cabinet in 2014, but not before she had helped to found the Free Enterprise Group of

Tory MPs. Sunak's political character was as it were existential. After Oxford he took a business degree at Stanford university in California, where he met his wife. He then worked for some years at Goldman Sachs and then for a couple of hedge funds. All in all, he was the personification of Theresa May's 'citizen of nowhere', the new class of super-rich.

Within the odiously demagogic overtones of May's words, there was a truth lurking. The class which knows no fatherland is the global plutocracy, and despite his doubtless sincere protestations of affection for the country of his birth, Sunak had joined that class, not so much because of the considerable sums he made himself working in finance as by his marriage. In the Victorian age, when the prime minister still appointed the senior offices in the Church of England – bishops, deans, archdeacons – a book was kept at Downing Street listing all the clergymen who might be suitable for preferment. Sometimes after the entry were written the initials 'w.h.m.', which stood for 'wife has means'. Sunak deserved 'w.h.m.' – and how. His wife, Akshata Narayana Murty, is the daughter of an Indian billionaire and herself hugely rich. It was an embarrassment for Sunak, and a perfectly legitimate criticism, when it was revealed that she was a 'non-dom', allowed the highly questionable privilege of residing in England while being domiciled elsewhere for tax purposes.

In the summer of 2022 these two took part in excruciating 'hustings' debates before the exiguous Tory party membership. When Margaret Thatcher was chosen as the Conservative candidate for Finchley in 1959, a senior member of the constituency Conservative Association complained the shortlist had offered them a choice between 'a bloody woman and a bloody Jew'. Choosing between another bloody woman and a bloody Hindu, the members voted decisively for the woman, thanks above all to her free-market pitch, and they got what they asked for.

Queen Elizabeth always spent late summer at Balmoral, the royal residence in Scotland, and on 6 September she had to receive first Johnson, who flew there to resign, then Truss, who arrived to be appointed his successor. Having to see the two of them in turn might be enough to polish off any frail ninety-six-year-old, and two days later the Queen died, closing a chapter more poignantly than any political changing of the guard, as the country lost the only head of state the overwhelming majority of the British people had ever known.

Returning to Westminster, Truss appointed as chancellor Kwasi Kwarteng, one of her closest political friends. In 2010 they were among a group of newly elected Tory MPs who published a book called *Britannia Unchained*, advocating a utopian (or dystopian) 'Singapore-on-Thames' of low taxes and minimal regulation, and containing the memorable words, 'The British are among the worst idlers in the world,' maybe not an ideal slogan for an election manifesto. On 23 September Kwarteng unveiled in Parliament his 'growth plan,' or scheme for unchaining, which proposed large tax cuts without any balancing reductions in public spending.

Rarely has any abstract political proposition been so quickly falsified. Sterling and government bonds plunged, as it turned out that, although the Truss government might have loved the markets, the markets did not love them. Kwasi Kwarcrash, as Alistair Osborne of *The Times* dubbed him, hung on for three weeks until 14 October, when Truss sacked him, in a desperate but unsuccessful attempt to save herself. At that point Starmer asked in the Commons, 'A book is being written about the prime minister's time in office. Apparently, it's going to be out by Christmas. Is that the release date or the title?' It turned out to be both.

On 19 October, Truss made her sorry last appearance in Parliament 2022, before resigning as prime minister after all of forty-nine days, beating George Canning's two-hundred-year-old record for the shortest premiership. It happened to be one hundred years to the day since Tory MPs voted to leave the coalition led by Lloyd George, who resigned immediately. That vote was also a repudiation of Austen Chamberlain, the Tory leader, and prompted A. J. Balfour's sour observation that 'it is not a principle of the Conservative Party to stab its leaders in the back, but I must confess that it often appears to be a practice'. By now practice had become addiction.

Citizen of Nowhere

Yet again, the Tory MPs contrived to short-circuit the ridiculous electoral system and, after other candidates dropped out, Sunak was chosen as leader by default. But what an inheritance he found! As if in the television series *Life on Mars*, we seemed to have been taken back fifty years to the 1970s and problems we'd hoped never to see again. Surely 'stagflation' was a thing of the past, but no, here it came once more: the United Kingdom now had both the lowest growth rate and one of the highest rates of inflation among advanced industrial nations.

It was the only Western country whose economy had not grown since the pandemic. At the beginning of 2023, the *Financial Times*'s annual survey of leading British economists was cheerlessly headlined 'UK faces worst and longest recession in G7, say economists'; and at the end of January the International Monetary Fund predicted that the British economy would perform worse that year than all other advanced economies, including Russia's.

Disposable incomes and living standards had been falling faster than for decades, and the Bank of England's latest rise in interest rates – the tenth consecutive increase – in early

February sent many mortgage payments up again. Not surprisingly, Christmas and the New Year saw a wave of strikes for higher pay, by border guards and railway, bus, and post office workers, bringing the country almost to a halt – and worse than that when they were joined by firefighters as well as nurses and ambulance drivers, aggravating the woes of the National Health Service, which is the object of so much patriotic pride but which now sometimes seems near collapse.

As if all those had not been problems enough for Sunak, he was still cleaning up the festering mess left behind by Johnson. At the end of January he sacked Nadhim Zahawi as chairman of the Conservative Party when it transpired that he had been evasive about a £1 million penalty he had been obliged to pay for a questionable tax return – and this at the very time when he was serving as chancellor of the Exchequer. Sunak was also under intense pressure to deal with Dominic Raab, the deputy prime minister and former foreign secretary, after multiple accusations that he bullied officials. Needless to say, Zahawi and Raab were both appointed by Johnson. Most Johnsonian of all had been the appointment of Richard Sharp as chairman of the BBC. Sharp is a rich former banker who spent most of his career at Goldman Sachs (for which Sunak also worked, like everyone else, it sometimes seems). He was once an adviser to Johnson, he has donated more than £400,000 to the Conservative Party, and when Johnson was at Downing Street Sharp helped facilitate a private loan of £800,000 for him.

When Sunak formed his cabinet it demonstrated if nothing else the Tories' continued capacity for reinvention:

whatever else they might be, they were plainly not a white nativist party. The first names of the latest four French finance ministers at that time were Bruno, Michel, Pierre, and François; of their German counterparts, Christian, Olaf, Peter, and Wolfgang; of American secretaries of the Treasury, Janet, Steven, Jack, and Timothy. The four successive chancellors of the Exchequer until the previous October were called Sajid, Rishi, Nadhim, and Kwasi. Bruno Maçães, the Portuguese politician who is now a prolific commentator, said that there is no other European country where four people with such names could all have risen to such a position.

Three of the highest offices – the premiership and the two historic secretaryships of state – were held by people of colour: the foreign secretary was James Cleverly, whose mother was from Sierra Leone, and the home secretary was Suella Braverman, whose parents were Indian by way of Mauritius and Kenya. Veneration of Churchill is a dogma of the Tory party, which chooses to overlook much that he did and said. He once told a colleague that 'the Hindus were a foul race' who deserved to be extirpated, and in 1955, at the last cabinet meeting over which he presided as prime minister, he said that the Tories should fight the next election on the slogan 'Keep England White'.

At the Conservative Party Conference the following year, one of the speakers was Captain Charles Waterhouse, a veteran of the Great War, an MP since the 1920s, and a great conference favourite. In his speech he used the phrase 'nigger in the woodpile'; added in a stage aside, 'Too many of them about anyway'; and brought the house down with raucous laughter. What Churchill would have made of a Hindu (and a teetotaller!) at 10 Downing Street scarcely bears thinking about. And yet it might not be sheer accident that the party that gave us a prime minister named Disraeli in 1868 and a prime minister named Margaret in 1979 (as well as two more women prime ministers since) should now give us one called Sunak.

He was by some way the richest man to be prime minister for many years, or possibly ever, depending on how money values are calculated. At least that kept Sunak free of the need to raise funds for himself from donors, as Johnson has done. The last period when British politics were genuinely corrupt was in the early decades of the last century. Lord Balcarres – later Earl of Crawford – was a connoisseur and collector, a Tory whip in the Commons, and a brilliantly observant diarist. In October 1912 he recorded, 'The common talk of the lobby and the City,' which was 'government corruption – personal corruption. The radicals seem to vie with one another in payment for honours and in recoupment via public contracts . . . These penniless ministers are not living at their extravagant rate upon the official salaries. Lloyd George is not building his new house out of his salary. Somebody must be funding him. Who, and above all, why?'

Rather more than ten years later his most flagrant sale of honours had helped bring down Lloyd George, and now that outrage returned. Apart from Truss, who wished quite preposterously to award an honour for every four days of her brief tenure, some startlingly improper peerages were handed out by Johnson. Along with his cronies such as Moore and Roberts, one new peer was Evgeny Lebedev, a shadowy oligarch and son of a KGB officer. But Johnson really had no need to worry, even after a messy and extremely expensive divorce from his second wife. In the five months after he was ejected from office he collected nearly £5 million. That included part of a multimillion-pound multibook deal that he struck personally when he visited Murdoch at his Arizona ranch, as well as fees for speeches he had given or is going to give in America.

Writing in the *New York Review of Books* only weeks after Sunak became prime minister, I said that not only he but everyone else had expressed a wish that 2023 should be an improvement on 2022. But I was haunted by the memory of the speech that the Albanian dictator Enver Hoxha made to his unfortunate people one January long ago: 'This year will be harder than last year. On the other hand, it will be easier than next year.'

And so it proved. As 2023 unfolded there was very little comfort for the Tories. Sunak's sobriety, or downright dullness, might have been refreshing contrast after the ludicrous pantomime that had preceded him at Downing Street. Politicians don't need to be charismatic or vivid to lead their parties to electoral victory. That was conclusively demonstrated in 1945 when Labour, led by the reticent and unobtrusive Attlee, won a landslide against a Tory party led by the most famous, flamboyant, and loquacious man on earth. Admittedly, Sir Keir Starmer is even duller than Sunak, but there were signs that the country had wearied of exuberance, and November brought warnings from elsewhere, with the electoral victories of two right-wing rabble-rousers, Javier Milei in Argentina and Geert Wilders in the Netherlands.

As the year wore on Sunak had even more reason for despondency, with more by-election losses. One of them was in Mid Bedfordshire, a seat vacated – at long last – by Nadine Dorries. She was exuberant enough, a working-class Liverpudlian and pure representative of the new Tory populism, even if the causes she had tried to promote as an MP, such as reducing the time limit for abortions and making sexual abstinence for girls part of the school curriculum, were not in fact very popular. And the latter would scarcely have suited Boris Johnson, to whom she attached herself politically.

He had made her culture secretary, an appointment that caused much merriment, but she resigned when Truss was chosen as party leader, and openly demanded to be given a peerage. When it did not come her way, Dorries went on strike, carrying out none of her Parliamentary duties until she was finally shamed into resigning her seat, not that shame was something she seemed to feel very often: her claims for Parliamentary expenses had been notably outrageous, showing that politicians had learned nothing from the scandal of 2009. Her last act, by way of vacating her seat, was to enable Labour not only to win but to overturn the largest Tory majority at any by-election since 1945.

Or rather that was her penultimate gesture. Her very final act of revenge was to publish an entirely preposterous book called *The Plot* about 'the political assassination of Boris Johnson'. This had been carried out, she said, as was the subsequent destruction of Liz Truss, by 'The Movement', a cabal including Michael Gove and Dominic Cummings, but led by 'Dr No', an immensely powerful figure with strange sexual appetites who had controlled the Conservative Party for forty years but who could not, sad to say, be named for legal reasons. This kind of claptrap might have been concocted by any half-cracked conspiracy theorist. That it was written by an erstwhile culture secretary in a Tory cabinet said far more about what had happened to the party than Dorries could possibly have realised.

One record in which the Tories could take justifiable pride, at least in an abstract sense, was that no fewer than three women had been leaders of the party and prime ministers. By contrast, Labour has never been led by a woman. But then again, the mere fact of appropriate chromosomes was no guarantee of true political ability or wisdom.

That truth was embodied by Suella Braverman. While noting the well-known phenomenon of the ultranationalism of the outsider – Napoleon was Corsican, Stalin was Georgian, Hitler was Austrian, and de Valera was Cuban – Orwell wondered whether, if England ever found a demagogic nationalist standard-bearer, that person might be likewise from the margins, maybe an Ulsterman. He didn't foresee a woman of Indian descent, her mother a Tamil by way of Mauritius and her father a Goan Christian born in Kenya, setting herself up as an English nativist tub-thumper. Having practised as a barrister with modest success, Braverman was elected to Parliament in 2015, and by 2022, when she belatedly joined in the calls for Johnson to resign, she was prominent and self-confident enough to stand for the leadership herself, before endorsing Liz Truss. In return Truss appointed her home secretary. Braverman then had to resign for sharing a confidential government document with a backbench Tory MP, but she was reappointed to the same office a week later by Sunak in return for her support.

More to the point she saw herself as the voice of the populist right, embracing in one package every one of its positions or prejudices. She was a Leaver who had chaired the ill-named European Research Group of backbench Brexotics. She strongly advocated sending asylum-seekers to Rwanda. She denounced, in a glorious phrase, '*Guardian*-reading tofu-eating wokerati', along with exponents of 'cultural Marxism', which last got her into trouble, since the phrase (whatever it might have meant) had been used by an anti-Semitic mass murderer.

Her reappointment by Sunak was on the principle enunciated with Texan bluntness by Lyndon Johnson: there was a kind of person you would rather have 'on the inside pissing out than on the outside pissing in'. Alas, Braverman micturated impartially outward and inward. Lord Melbourne had famously told his cabinet that it didn't matter what they said, as long as they all said the same thing. This tradition was ignored by more and more Tory ministers who conducted personal campaigns without the agreement or even knowledge of their cabinet colleagues.

At a complete loss as to how to deal with illegal immigration, what the government had come up with is a proposal which would have seemed absurdly far-fetched in a satirical novel: immigrants claiming asylum would be sent to Rwanda, a country in the heart of tropical Africa which had witnessed an appalling act of mass murder less than thirty years earlier. 'Satire is dead,' Tom Lehrer had said when Henry Kissinger was awarded the Nobel Peace Prize, but satire kept coming back from the dead to die again.

In April Braverman came up with a proposal to lodge 500 asylum-seekers in a barge by the unlikely name of *Bibby Stockholm*. But in the autumn the home secretary really turned up the volume. After the murderous attack by Hamas on 7 October, she denounced the large demonstrations in favour of the Palestinian people as 'hate marches', claimed that 'senior police officers play favourites when it comes to protesters' and were tougher on right-wing extremists than pro-Palestinian 'mobs', and told police to treat these demonstrations as a 'racially aggravated public order offence'. This came to a head when she published an article espousing these views in *The Times*, without first clearing it with Downing Street as ministers are required to do. Even a prime minister as weak as Sunak couldn't tolerate this insubordination without seeming even weaker. Braverman was sacked and James Cleverly was moved to the Home Office. And who should replace him as foreign secretary? The rabbit Sunak pulled out of his hat was, of all people, David Cameron, swiftly elevated as Lord Cameron of Chipping Norton.

Some Tories expressed mixed feelings about the reshuffle. The man Charles Moore liked to call 'Jacob Rees-Mogg, our future leader' said that 'getting rid of Suella is a mistake' because she had become 'identified in the public mind as someone who wanted to deal with the immigration problem and somebody who was tough on law and order'. On the other hand, Cameron's return was welcome: 'I'm delighted of course to have an Old Etonian back in the cabinet,' Rees-Mogg said. 'It was always very remiss not to have one.'

That was to overlook one or two problems. Since resigning as prime minister in the wake of the referendum, Cameron had followed Blair's example by devoting himself to making money. He was paid a large advance for his tedious memoir. Then it transpired that he had been lobbying ministers, his former colleagues, notably Sunak when he was chancellor, on behalf of a shadowy finance company called Greensill Capital. When he became foreign secretary, it was revealed that Cameron had also been helping a Chinese investment company.

There might have been a case for placing a former prime minister in the Foreign Office. That had happened before. Years after A. J. Balfour resigned as prime minster in 1905 he served as foreign secretary in Lloyd George's coalition from 1916 to 1919 (and signed the fateful Balfour Declaration in November 1917), and Sir Alec Douglas-Home, after his brief spell as prime minister in 1963–64 and succession as Tory leader by Edward Heath in 1965 had returned as foreign secretary in Heath's 1970–74 government. But even if Cameron's frantic money-grubbing weren't enough to disqualify him from this return to office there was his political record. At the first Prime Minister's Question Time after the appointment, a Labour backbencher asked Sunak politely if he could name Lord Cameron's foreign policy achievements, which produced a roar of laughter and almost silenced the prime minister. His 'achievements' ranged, of course, from the intervention in Libya with such catastrophic consequences to calling the referendum he didn't want to call but then expected to win, and lost.

Just after this game of musical chairs, Jeremy Hunt, the chancellor, gave a plausible imitation of sober statesmanship in his autumn statement, more accurately a budget. His reduction of the employees' contribution to National Insurance (which has long been fraudulent name to disguise another form of income tax) might even have hinted at a spring election. But there was a sense of too little, too late. Hunt's statement coincided unhappily with the news that real disposable household income per person was projected to be 3.5 per cent lower in 2024–25 than it was before the pandemic, which the Office for Budget Responsibility described as the 'largest reduction in real living standards since . . . records began in the 1950s'.

As if that weren't enough, the Office for National Statistics revealed that 'net migration' to the United Kingdom (which meant actual immigration when the numbers of emigrants was deducted from the total of immigrants) had been 745,000 to the year ending December 2022, the highest ever. The egregious Braverman called this figure 'a slap in the face' to the British public, and it was certainly a painful embarrassment to the Tories, most of all to her own gaggle of Brexotics.

Endgame

Only as we reached the third decade of the twenty-first century did we fully realise just how bad the opening two decades had been. The first saw Labour in office, and the worst crimes of the Blair government became clearer as time passed, whether it was the full scale of his perfidy and mendacity when taking the country into the Iraq war, or the 2005 Gambling Act, which we now know ruined many lives by encouraging addictive online betting and allowed one woman who started an online gambling business in a garden shed to pay herself a salary of more than £250 million a year.

Had the Tories opposed or even vigorously criticised these things, they would have been in a far stronger position when they returned to office in 2010. But, to the contrary, they were inspired by a spirit of emulation, in terms of governing, and of corruption, on a scale we have gradually come to recognise. Only a very innocent spirit would think British politics had always been free of any taint of financial impropriety. Politics in the eighteenth century were thoroughly corrupt, and later in the following century Gladstone bought Egyptian stock shortly before his government attacked Egypt in 1882, and Salisbury invested in a company making small warships which his government would buy. By the twentieth century Lloyd George took the practice of selling honours to a degree so flagrant it helped end his career.

That abuse was meant to have been stopped by the 1925 Honours (Prevention of Abuses) Act, but recently the award of honours to large party donors has again become outrageous. And there were other types of corruption besides. The 'revolving door' has long been a feature of political life, permitting free movement between government and the lucrative private sector. In the past, prime ministers and other politicians were expected to make some money from writing their memoirs or maybe accepting company directorships, and in any case backbench MPs have always been free to pursue other careers, as barristers, journalists, businessmen or trade union secretaries. As much to the point, most MPs sat in parliament without expectation of office, which was statistically unlikely. In 1900, there were 670 MPs, of whom no more than thirty-three were salaried members of the government; by 2000 eighty-two of 659 MPs were ministers of one sort or another and by now there are over 110, along with a quite absurd increase in the number of Parliamentary private secretaries from nine to forty-seven, the unpaid bag-carriers expected to vote loyally with the government.

But then something quite new happened. Blair's departure from the prime ministership and Parliament on the same day immediately to take up positions with banks and finance companies paying him several millions a year was truly unprecedented. In Alan Bennett's lethal phrase, for Blair, politics had been no more than a booster rocket taking him in to the financial stratosphere. Tories of another age might have looked on this with disdain. Instead, they saw it as an example. Cameron had billed himself 'Blair's heir' and Osborne called Blair 'the Master'. They surely learned from him when they both left office, following the Brexit referendum. Osborne collected his grotesque £650,000 a year for one day's work a week, which was at least publicly known.

It only later transpired that Cameron had been surreptitiously lobbying ministers – his former colleagues – for a shadowy company called Greensill, which collapsed in scandalous circumstances. A Commons committee said meiotically that he had shown 'a lack of judgement'. He didn't show much more judgement when he bestowed a peerage on Michelle Mone, whose business made exotic women's underwear. When the pandemic struck she helped secure her husband a contract to produce PPE, much of which turned out to be faulty, although the family trust was still enriched by tens of millions.

In 2015, Xi Jinping, the Chinese president, paid a state visit to England. Cameron took him for a matey pint in pub near Chequers, while Osborne, still chancellor, said that Anglo-Chinese relations had entered a 'golden era'. The phrase was taken up by Cameron and, out of office, he forged new financial contacts with China, while both he and Osborne built further financial ties to the Gulf states. In another age that would surely have ended any hope of a continued political career. Instead, when Sunak summoned to the Foreign Office 'Lord Slippery of Tripoli', as Peter Hitchens dubbed Cameron, recalling his disastrous Libyan venture, it only turned more light on his financial career during the seven years he had been out of office.

Even Tory newspapers were dismayed. The *Daily Mail* asked, 'Just how much has our Foreign Secretary David Cameron been making in the Middle East? And why are his deals being kept secret?' The *Daily Telegraph* had long occupied a unique position as the most solid and sane supporter of the Conservative Party and Conservative governments, under the ownership of the Berry family. In 1985, beset by the woes that ailed all Fleet Street, in particular intransigent printing unions, Lord Hartwell, the head of the family, lost control of the paper to Canadian entrepreneur Conrad Black.

But he in turn lost control to the twin brothers David and Frederick Barclay, shadowy businessmen and tax exiles, whose own problems led the *Daily Telegraph*, its sister the *Sunday Telegraph*, and the weekly *Spectator*, which they also now owned, to be placed on the market. The leading bidder was a hedge fund whose chief investor was the sovereign wealth fund of Abu Dhabi. While journalists on the papers volubly protested that no national newspaper should be controlled by a foreign state, let alone an autocracy where freedom of the press was almost unknown, it came as no surprise at all to learn that Osborne had been acting as an adviser to the would-be purchasers.

If that had lost the power to shock, another frightful scandal only fully entered public consciousness thanks to a television docudrama. For years many hundreds of sub-postmasters had been falsely accused of fraud, in many cases convicted, often financially ruined, some of them imprisoned and a few tragically driven to suicide. All this was because of a faulty computer system in which the Post Office management placed blind faith, followed by a mendacious cover-up. Very few people in public life or the media emerged with much credit. National newspapers now waxed indignant, although they had done little enough at the time. The journals who tried to expose the scandal from early on, to little avail, were *Computer Weekly* and *Private Eye*.

Once the public was enraged by this horror, politicians inevitably joined in, but almost none had done anything before. One who did and came out of the story with a spotless or even heroic reputation was James Arbuthnot, now Lord Arbuthnot. He had sat as a Conservative MP from 1987 to 2015, never rising above junior office although he served as chairman of the Defence Select Committee, when he was able to right another wrong, by exonerating the pilot of an RAF helicopter which had crashed in Scotland in 1994, killing most of the British government's senior intelligence officials working in Northern Ireland.

He took up the case of the sub-postmasters early on and persevered despite all discouragement. Even now Arbuthnot had the humility to say that 'I failed', which was true inasmuch as the scandal was never acknowledged for many years however hard he tried. Son of a baronet, educated at Eton and Cambridge, a barrister by original trade (as was his wife, who became a High Court judge), what was so striking about Arbuthnot was that he seemed a revenant, an almost unique survival from a distant age when the old upper class still sometimes produced worthy public men and women, and when the Conservative Party actually contained honourable and decent politicians, rather than chancers and money-grubbers.

Even if Sunak had originally offered sheer relief after his predecessors, by the end of his first year as prime minister he seemed increasingly out of his depth. In October, the *Daily Express*, a shadow of what it had been in its heyday, selling four million copies but now acting as a faithful stooge to the government, splashed the headline 'PM: I'll tear up rulebook of 30 years of broken politics'. On this occasion Osborne was right, not to say stating the obvious, when he said that Sunak couldn't 'pull off being the change candidate'. Change from what? From thirty years for most of which the Conservatives have been in office?

Not surprisingly there were intermittent calls for Sunak to be replaced, and even talk of plots to do so, although the slowest-witted Tory must have sensed that to depose a fourth leader in five years would destroy the faintest pretense they were a serious party. But still, there was an increasing air of desperation when Sunak spoke. Early in his prime minister-ship he had made five 'pledges', which common sense would have told him were unlikely to be met and were anyway beyond his control, notably his promises to reduce inflation and NHS waiting lists. Indeed by February 2024 he admit-ted that the waiting lists had not come down.

Another policy was always doomed to backfire. A delete-rious recent development was the lectern outside 10 Downing Street adorned with the latest fatuous slogan, latterly 'Stop the boats.' As everyone could see, the boats crossing the Channel had not been stopped, and the government's boasted stratagem for deterring them had come to nothing. In 1994 an unseemly joke could be heard in Washington: 'Mr President, what are we going to do about Rwanda?' 'That Rwanda's a lying bitch. I never laid a finger on her.' But now Rwanda became a bad joke in British politics, with the government's weird plan to deport asylum seekers to a remote tropical African country whose human rights record even now was such that England was admitting asylum seekers from Rwanda, the country to which it was proposing to send asylum seekers. In February Sunak was interviewed on television by the bumptious Piers Morgan, who bet the prime minister £1,000 that no one would have been deported to Rwanda before the election. Sunak had little choice but to accept and console himself that it will be easier for him to pay up than it would be for most citizens.

Through all this turmoil the Tories were ailed by something they couldn't shake off. Margaret Thatcher was an astonishing creature who dominated a whole decade, who changed the country, who could be called a world-historical figure. Even after her eviction in 1990, her shadow fell for many years over Labour governments as much as Tory. The malady from which the Tories now suffer is of a different character. If some patients unluckily suffer from 'long Covid', when the effects of the virus linger, the Tories were afflicted by 'long Boris'. They had known what he was like when they chose him as a leader. They cheered his initial victories, they watched with dismay his hopeless incompetence when the pandemic came, and they finally ejected him, not because he was a scoundrel, which they knew anyway, but because everyone else could now see that he was.

He continued to heckle from the sidelines by way of a column in the *Daily Mail* for which he was paid not much less than £1 million a year, and it was the same old same old, the perky, fatuous performance he had been putting on for twenty-five years, entirely devoid of any sense of public duty while delighting in the idea of Big Things he might have done: 'Cancel HS2? Cut off the northern leg? We must be out of our minds . . . Opponents said Australia's small boats plan was cruel and crackers . . . until it worked. The same will happen with Rwanda . . . Rugby doesn't risk young people's lives, it can *save* them. Don't let the finger-wagging twaddle merchants of Weedy-Wetsville University tell you other-wise . . . Why can't every freeborn Briton burn his Christmas tree on Twelfth Night in his own hearth?' and so on and on.

A particularly odious example was a column praising the good old spirit of adventure and love of the unknown which had been exemplified in the last dive of the submersible called *Titan*. This scandalous affair saw a millionaire not only book himself aboard an unseaworthy craft but cajole his nineteen-year-old son, who hadn't wanted to go, to join him in a terrifying death and in a watery grave, as it proved. What sort of person could admire that father?

Even when appearing in *Putin vs the West*, the latest of Norma Percy's brilliant television documentary series, in which many other leaders spoke gravely and seriously, John-son couldn't help smirking as he described his telephone conversations with Xi. 'He kept dead-batting. More dead bats than in a Yuhan cave.' By early 2024 it was increasingly likely Donald Trump would win the American presidential election in November, and even more likely that if he did so he would abandon Ukraine. And yet Johnson could write another column in his inimitable, not to say ineffable, manner: 'The global wokerati are trembling so violently you can hear the ice tinkling in their negronis . . . but a Trump presi-dency could be just what the world needs.' That entirely contradicted another column – 'Our support for Israel is as important as that for Ukraine' – which at least provided comic relief with its joint byline of Boris Johnson and Bernard-Henri Lévy neatly pairing two of the prize preening boobies of the age.

In February there were by-elections in two safe Tory seats, except that 'safe Tory seat' was by now what logicians call a closed category, like 'a square circle'. The Wellingborough by-election had been forced by accusations of bullying and sexual misconduct against Peter Bone, the sitting member, and then a recall petition, and the new Tory candidate appeared to be his partner or mistress or whatever the latest Tory term is. Even the prime minister couldn't be persuaded to say that he would vote Tory himself in that by-election, but party optimists could bet on the Tories retaining both seats at combined odds of an 89–1 double.

A hackneyed old phrase had once said that the Tories were a 'broad church', although that must be true of any party under the present British electoral system, which encourages large parties with the character of internal coalitions. But now the Tories seemed less a church than a variety of squabbling sects. It was hard to keep up with them: One Nation, New Conservatives, European Research Group (the innocuously named faction which had been driving force behind Brexit), Common Sense Group (which sounded almost contradictory in the present Tory party), National Conservatives. Those last held a conference in London in the spring of 2023 where some of the then darlings of the Tory Right appeared, such as Michael Gove, Jacob Rees-Mogg, the historian David Starkey for light relief, and Suella Braverman, who said that large-scale immigration undermined the 'national character'. She might also almost have been giving a practical demonstration, since she, the daughter of immigrants, had conspicuously failed to acquire that well-known English characteristic, a sense of irony.

Finally there popped up the Popular Conservatives, launched in February under the banner and leadership of Liz Truss, which again suggested a lack of any sense of the ridiculous after her brief but disastrous prime ministership. Apart from her, its first event was graced by Sir Jacob Rees-Mogg and the former deputy chairman, Lee Anderson, personifying respectively the would-be gentlemanly side of Toryism and its brutish foul-mouthed saloon-bar wing. Nigel Farage was in the audience, but then he was everywhere, haunting the tour wherever they turned. More dangerous in electoral terms was the new Reform Party, very much the latest incarnation of Ukip, which had already briefly been transmogrified as the Brexit Party. Its animating force was Richard Tice, a rich businessman, and its main attraction was Nigel Farage. Reform intends to run candidates in as many constituencies as possible and can only draw support from disaffected Tories.

There was even talk of Farage joining the Conservatives. Several Tories insisted that was unthinkable, but Rees-Mogg said he would be delighted. He had also welcomed the return of Cameron, claiming it was good to have an Etonian in the Cabinet again: 'It was very remiss not to have one.' But then another Etonian MP was Danny Kruger, an evangelical Christian, who had earlier claimed that the Tories needed to introduce 'a period of creative destruction in the public services'. If that wasn't much help to Sunak, then nor was Kruger's latest quite plausible lament that the Tory government would leave the country 'sadder, less united and less conservative than they had found it'.

That the Conservatives would be leaving the country, or at least office, was something very few disputed by the spring of 2024. They were spooked by Reform UK, the latest iteration of Nigel Farage's destructive political career, whose threat to run a candidate in every constituency would certainly be ruinous for the Tories. Many Tory MPs expected to lose their seats and were making plans for the future – the latest to say he was leaving as I write was Kwasi Kwarteng, perhaps hoping that his thirty-eight days as chancellor would be an attraction for future employers – while predictions for the party's prospects at the coming election ranged from dismal to disastrous. No one could possibly thrill at the thought of the coming Labour government. Sir Keir Starmer, like Blair before him, had decided that his best course was to track the Tories to the right, if not quite so far, and shied away from any hint of radicalism. But if ever the old saw of British politics applied, that oppositions don't win elections, governments lose them, then the coming election looked like a very clear demonstration of this truth.

And so to go back to the beginning and to my subtitle, whatever had happened to the Tory party? It is by any standards an extraordinary political phenomenon, not so much the possibly misleading fact that something called a Tory party existed for three and a half centuries as that the Tories had confounded so many fond hopes of a radical or socialist twentieth century. But it had done so by avoiding blind reaction and extreme nationalism of a kind which would plague Europe during much of that century. It might have been the party of capital, but it accepted and even fostered state welfare.

Part of the problem has been the undoubted degeneration of the party in terms of personnel. It would be sentimental to suppose that all Tory politicians of the past had been exemplary characters, but the party does recently seem to have attracted more than its fair share of scoundrels, cheats and sexual eccentrics. One Palermo newspaper used to have a daily page of smaller news items under the general heading 'La Sicilia Violente', and a London paper could now have a regular future: 'Tory Scandal Latest'. By the new year of 2024 it counted as good news for the Tories if one of their MPs was not after all going to be prosecuted for rape. On 15 February, we learned that the British economy had contracted for the last two successive quarters and was now in recession, but for Sunak this was a case of 'The worst is not / So long as we can say, "This is the worst."' That same day the Tories lost two by-elections to Labour, at Wellingborough, where they had had a majority of more than 18,000 votes at last election, and at Kingswood, where their majority had been more than 11,000. In both seats Reform UK came third, and a quarter of those who voted Tory in 2019 say they now support Reform. In Liz Truss's forlornly meiotic recent words, 'It's difficult being a Conservative at the moment.'

Above all the Tories had traditionally held back from fanaticism, or simply from ideology. Conservatism has many grave vices, but it, and in particular English Toryism, had certain redeeming virtues: pragmatism, scepticism, pessimism, and sheer common sense. Those virtues have occasionally deserted the Tories, as in the years before the Great War when Ireland drove them mad. A hundred years later they were driven mad again, by Europe. It was not the fact of Brexit, not even the economic damage it had obviously caused, so much as the political consequences for the Tories, both the party and the Tory press.

That press had changed far more over fifty years than most people now recognise. The *Daily Telegraph* under Lord Camrose and his son Lord Hartwell had been staid, grey, even dull, but notably honest and even-handed: Camrose used to rebuke his editors, saying that a lead story read like a hand-out from Conservative Central Office. Today it is as hysterical as the *Daily Mail*, while the *Spectator* now bears no resemblance to the sophisticated, witty journal which Alexander Chancellor edited in the 1970s, which I was lucky enough to work for, and which would never have published today's bestiary of cranks and crackpots. Not surprisingly the calamity was personified by Johnson, who had written for the *Telegraph* and edited the *Spectator*, and whom the Tories chose even though they knew him to be an unprincipled mountebank who didn't even believe in the Brexit which would send him to Downing Street.

He was obviously not someone who could invoke past glories in any convincing way, as some of his colleagues might have liked, whispering the last enchantments of the 1950s. And nor could he invoke the best political traditions. In 1914, a Tory party which was supposed to stand for the constitution, legality and duty came near to inciting civil war and mutiny. In 2019, a party which, if it stood for anything, should have stood for parliamentary government and the rule of law brutally attacked both of them. In 1957, the great American essayist Dwight Macdonald looked back wistfully on his revolutionary-socialist days twenty years before, and added that 'the revival of a true, principled conservatism – not the bully-boy adventurism of McCarthy or the Suez Group – would be of the greatest value today'. And so it would be now: not the bully-boy adventurism of the European Research Group or 'National Conservatives' but just true, principled conservatism. At present that seems far too much to hope for.